IMAGES
of America

PLYMOUTH

IMAGES
of America

PLYMOUTH

Plymouth Historical Society

ARCADIA
PUBLISHING

ISBN 978-0-7385-5776-2

Published by Arcadia Publishing
Charleston, South Carolina

Printed in the United States of America

Library of Congress Catalog Card Number: 2008922471

For all general information contact Arcadia Publishing at:
Telephone 843-853-2070
Fax 843-853-0044
E-mail sales@arcadiapublishing.com
For customer service and orders:
Toll-Free 1-888-313-2665

Visit us on the Internet at www.arcadiapublishing.com

Contents

INTRODUCTION

The confluence of two major rivers, the Pemigewasset and the Asquamchumauke (now known as the Baker), in the center of New Hampshire was for a long time the stopping-off place for the Abanaki Indians on their travels between Canada and the seacoast. It is understandable then that given the natural waterways into the deep interiors of the state, white settlers would choose the same area to establish and incorporate the town of Plymouth in 1763. The rich soils of the river intervales supported productive farms, the forests of the surrounding hills provided lumber for trade and building, and the streams feeding into the two rivers gave power to a wide variety of mills. Plymouth has long since grown into a town devoted to business, education, and tourism—one which became a center for the growing population in the developing area. It is thanks to the endeavors of farsighted and imaginative citizens that Plymouth has grown and prospered and adapted over the past 225 years, as well as becoming a mecca for writers and poets in its day.

The advent of the railroad, reaching Plymouth and the Pemigewasset and Baker Rivers in 1850, ended the days of stagecoaches, which had plied the growing network of turnpikes in the region and brought a new surge of commerce and vacationers. The stagecoaches were also credited with strengthening ties to the cosmopolitan influences of Boston and New York. For 100 years, the railroad industry was an immense influence on the town, finally giving way to trucking and private automobiles.

But it is not the intent of this book to narrate a history of Plymouth. Rather, it is to provide glimpses of what the town looked like in various phases from a collection of photographs covering a period from roughly the 1860s to the 1960s. While not a comprehensive coverage of Plymouth's many faces, these photographs of changes and events serve to underscore the vitality and dynamics which have always been present in Plymouth and in its people. With the publication of this book, the Plymouth Historical Society has endeavored to communicate a sense of the past, which has resulted in the town we have today.

One

Main Street

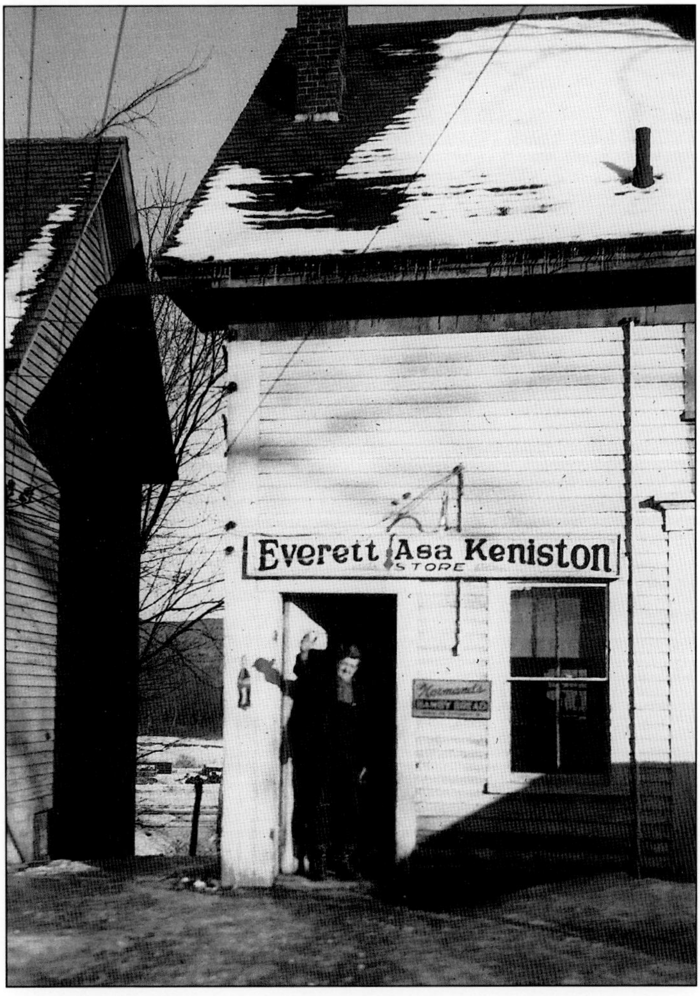

Everett Asa Keniston's hearty wave from the doorway of his well-known store on South Main Street exemplified the welcome that locals and visitors alike have received in downtown Plymouth for many years.

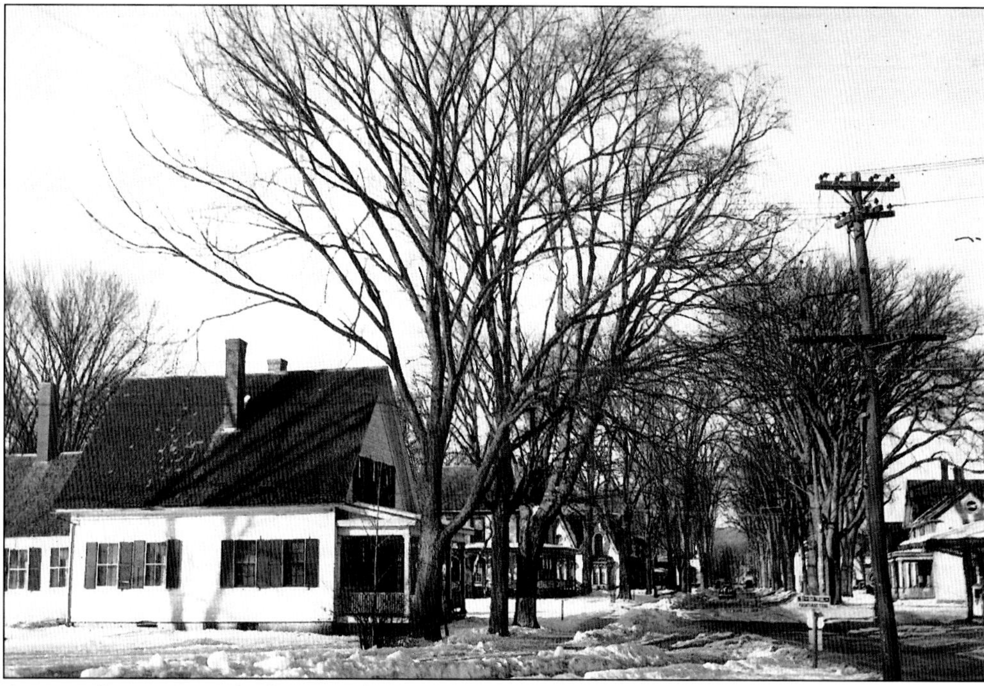

A view of Main Street looking north from Warren Street in the 1930s shows some of Plymouth's abundant elm trees. The trees would stand for several more years before succumbing to hurricanes and Dutch elm disease.

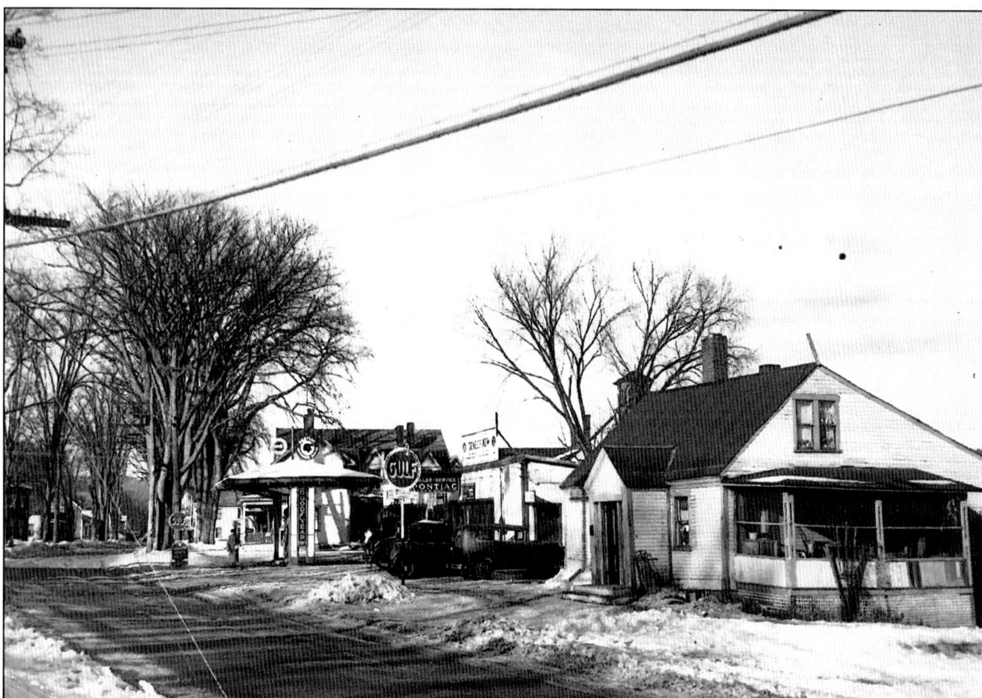

The Tree House Restaurant now stands where the Pontiac Sales and Service garage was operated.

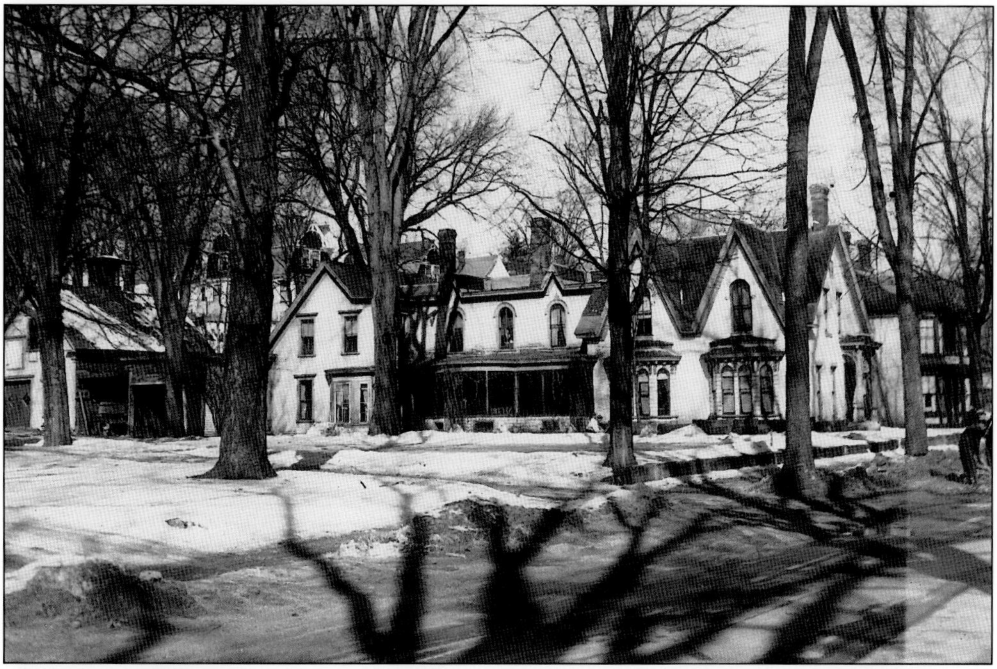

The stately William Dodge home was located on the present site of the Rite-Aid parking lot.

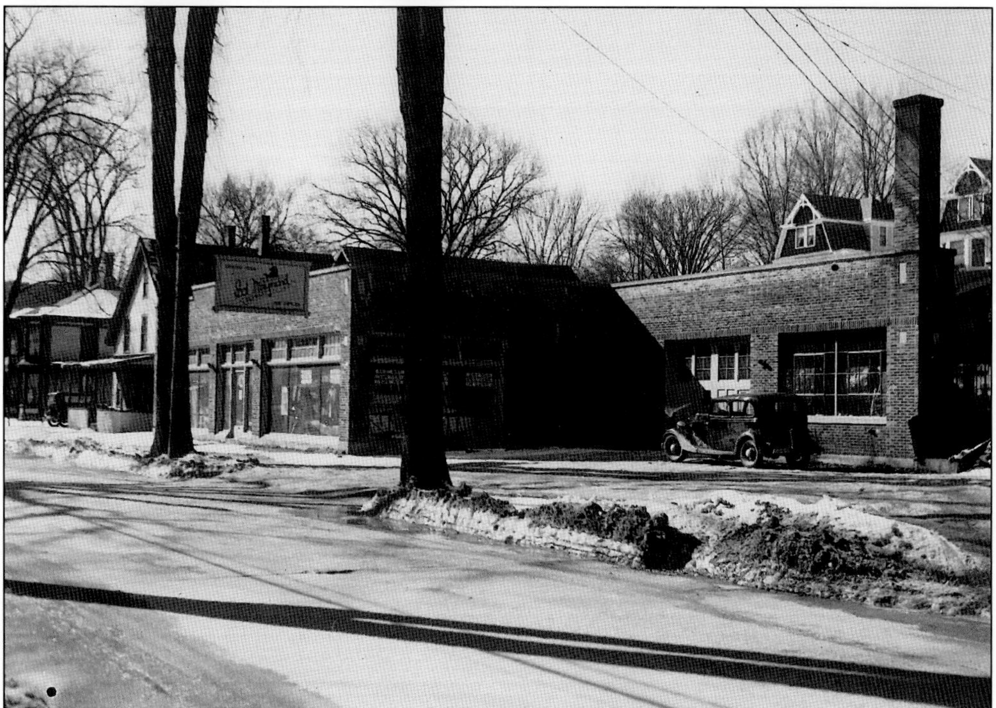

Originally built as a Buick showroom, this building has housed at various times the Plymouth Post Office, Ed Maynard's sports store, and Heal's Plymouth/Dodge dealership and garage. It was remodeled in the 1980s and now houses the Community Guaranty Savings Bank and Western Auto store.

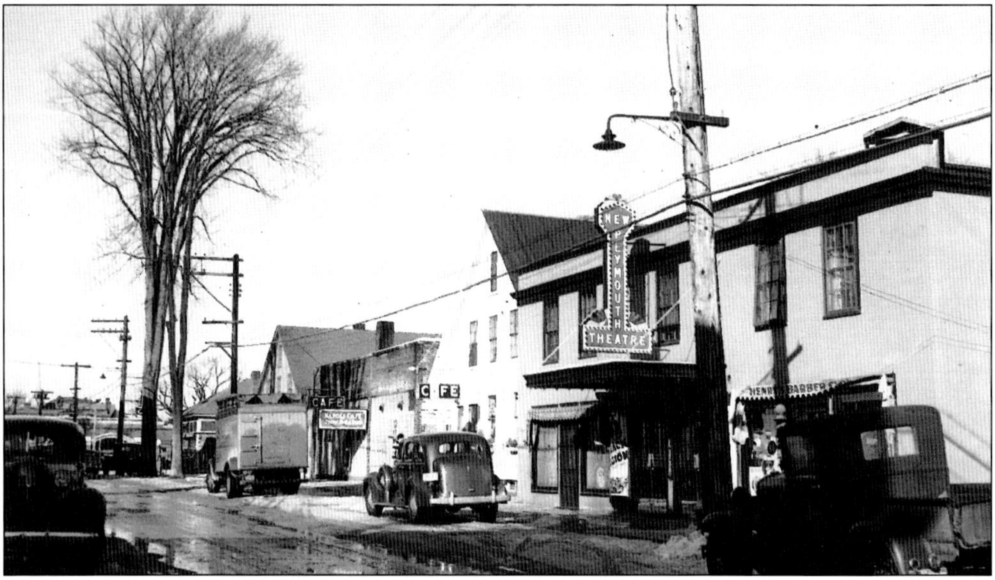

This photo of the "old" New Plymouth Theater shows some still familiar landmarks on Main Street, including the Napoli Cafe, later known as Fausty's.

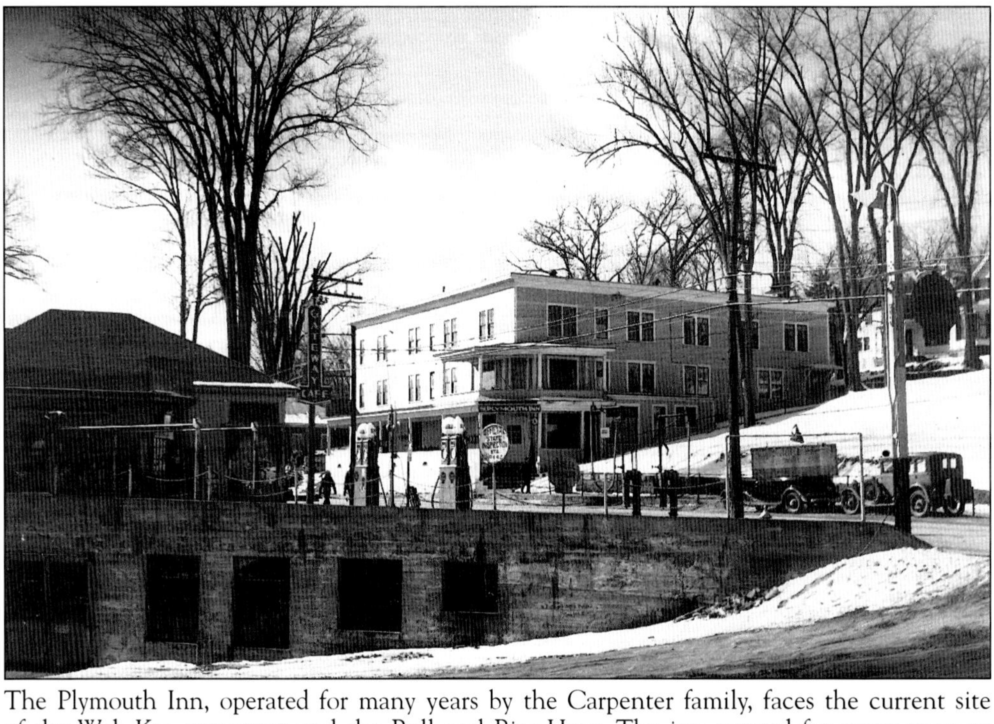

The Plymouth Inn, operated for many years by the Carpenter family, faces the current site of the Wah-Kee restaurant and the Bull and Bier Haus. The inn catered for many years to traveling businessmen and area tourists, also providing its clientele and local families with an excellent dining room.

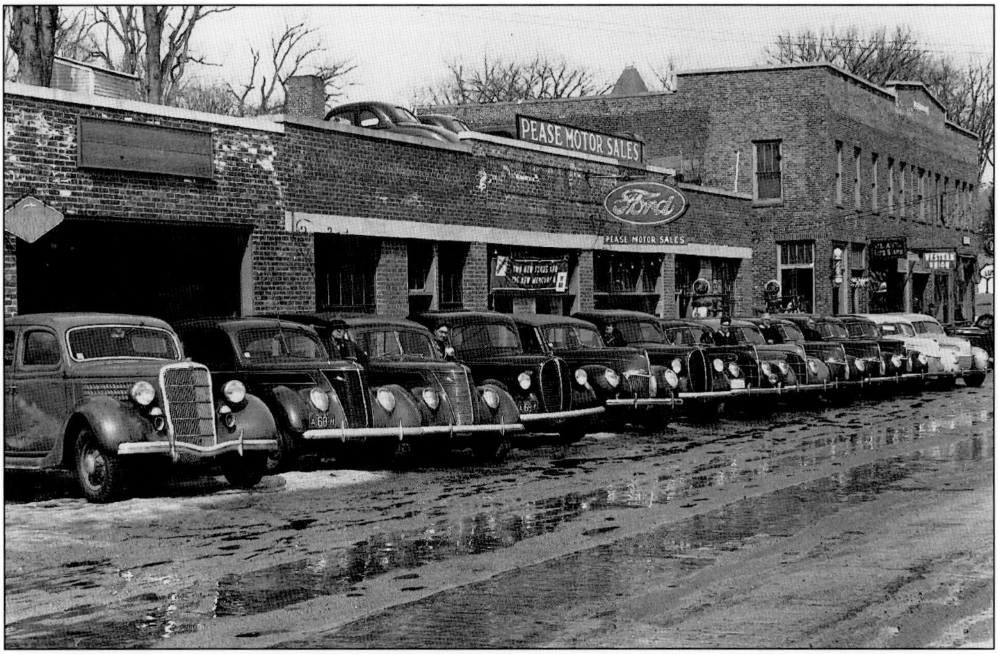

Pease Motor Sales was bustling in 1937; 20 new cars were sold during a 10-day March sale.

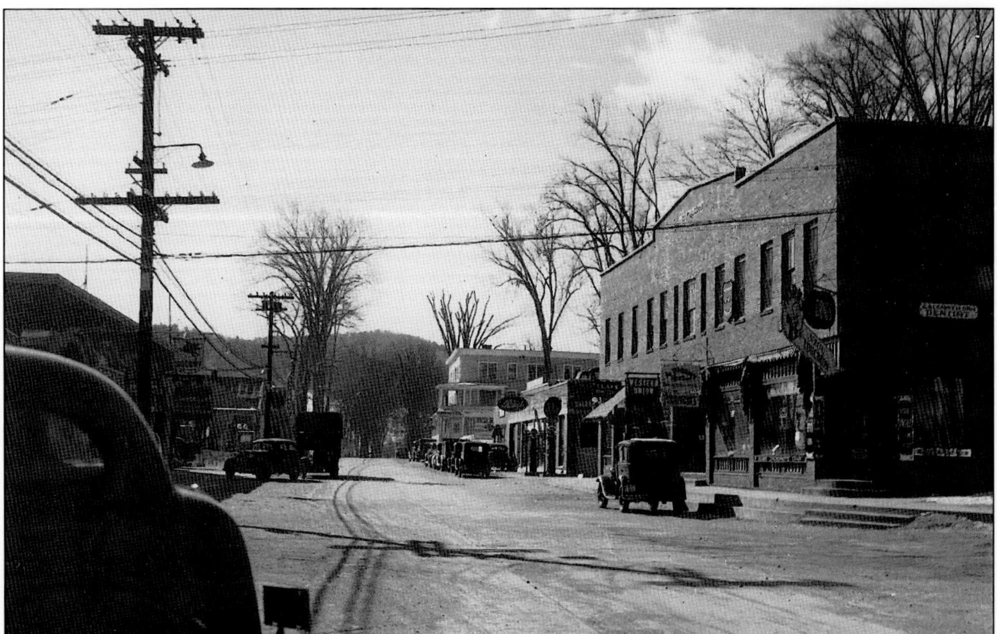

Destroyed by fire in 1895, the Plummer Fox Store was replaced by a three-story brick store. After this building also burned on December 3, 1929, the two-story brick building above was erected. It remains standing today as the Fox Block.

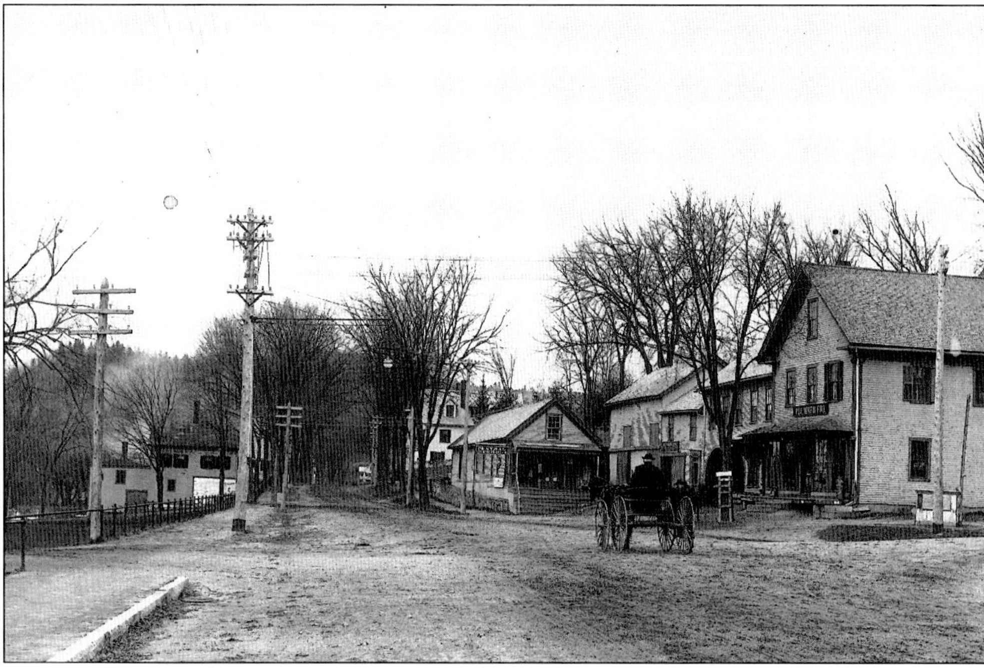

This view of Main Street looking south shows the original Plummer Fox Store at the corner of Highland Street before it burned in 1895.

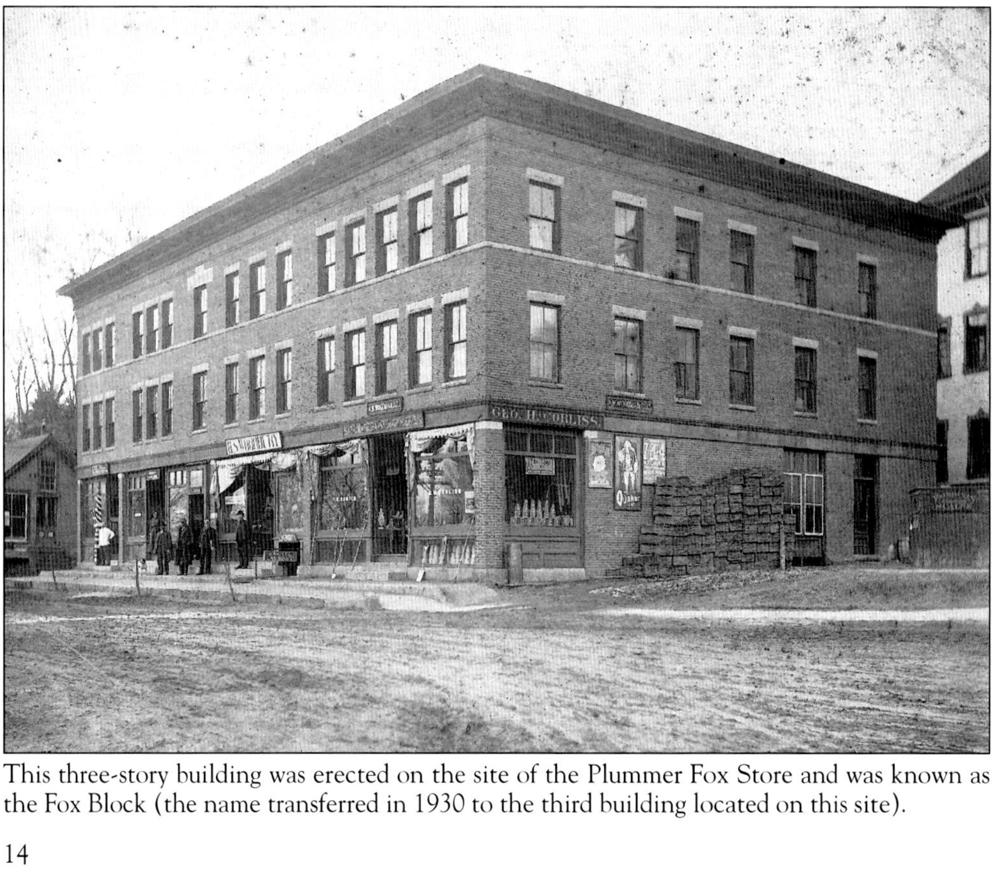

This three-story building was erected on the site of the Plummer Fox Store and was known as the Fox Block (the name transferred in 1930 to the third building located on this site).

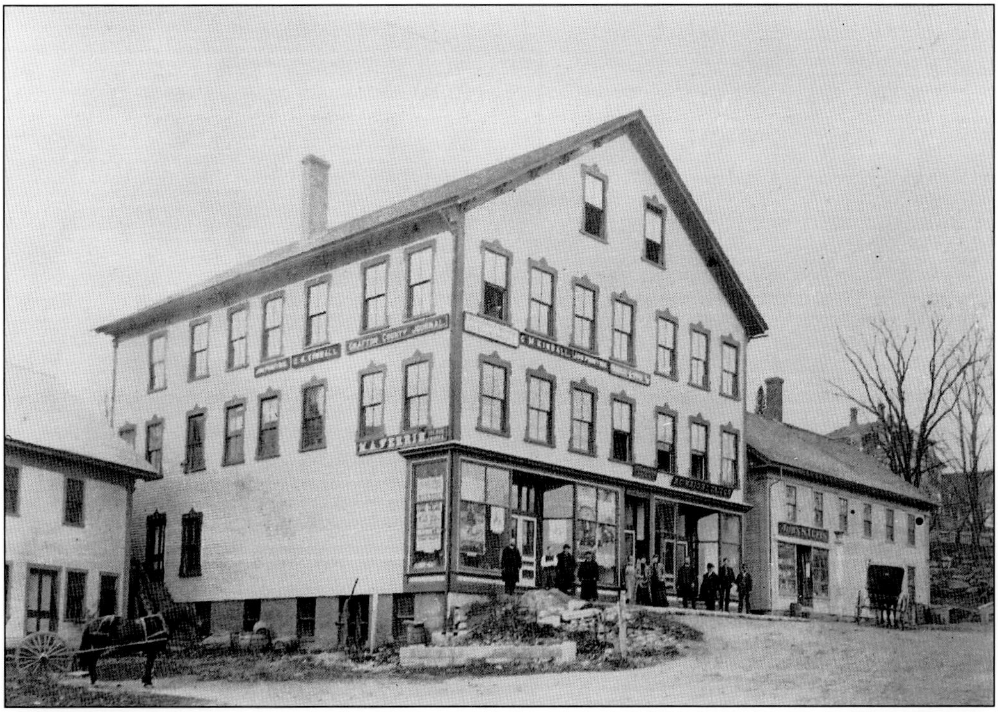

Also destroyed in the fire of December 3, 1929, was the Tufts Block, now the site of the Pemigewasset National Bank. The heat reflected by the rock ledge behind the building forced onlookers back as far as Court Street.

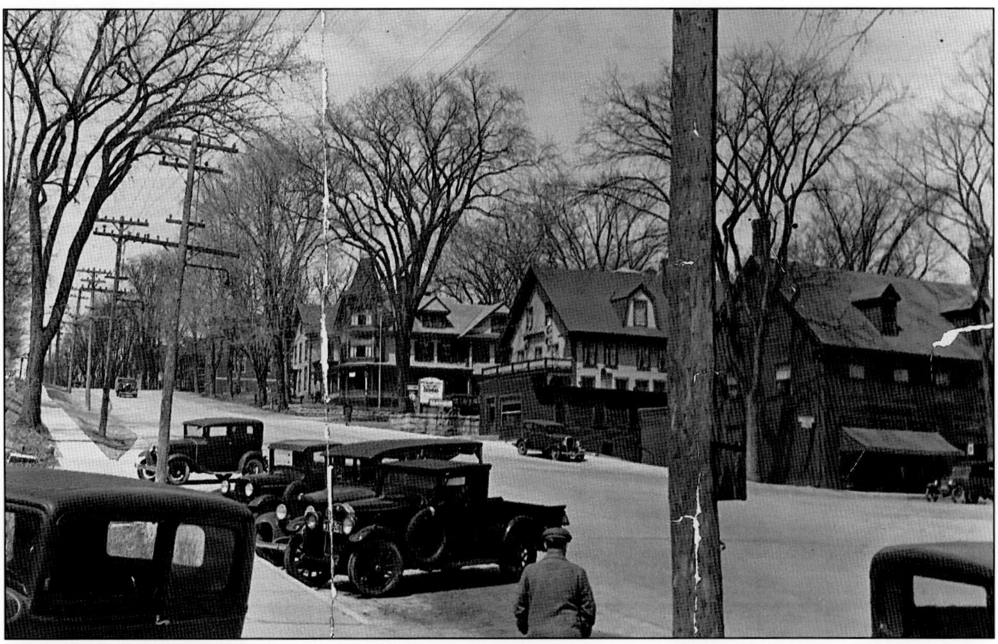

This view of Highland Street from the corner of Main Street in the early 1930s is quite different from today's scene. Many of the elm trees were downed in the Hurricane of 1938.

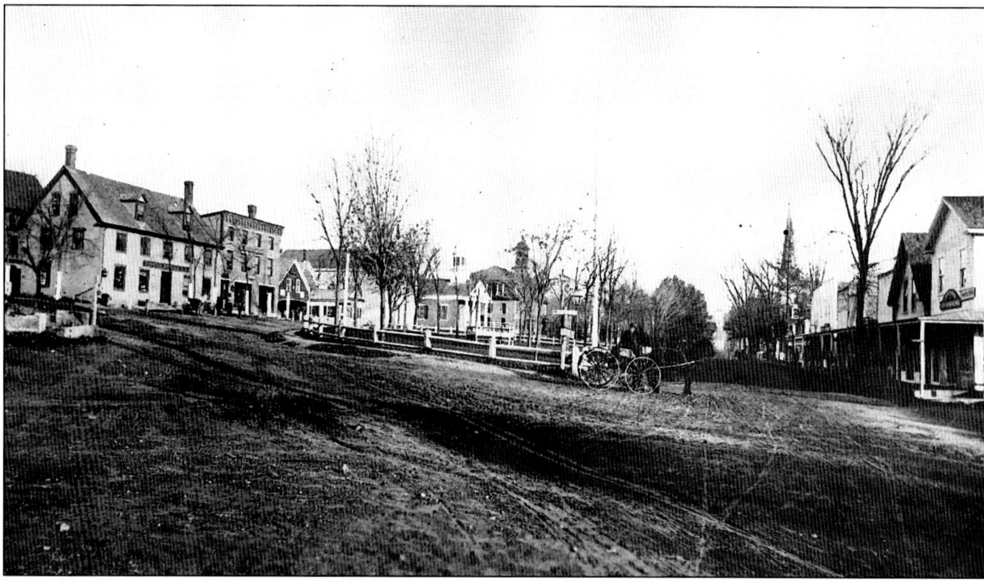

Russell Square, as the downtown Common area was known in the 1870s, has unpaved streets, gas lamps, and a new fence around the Common proper. The row of wooden buildings on the right was known as the "Ten Footers."

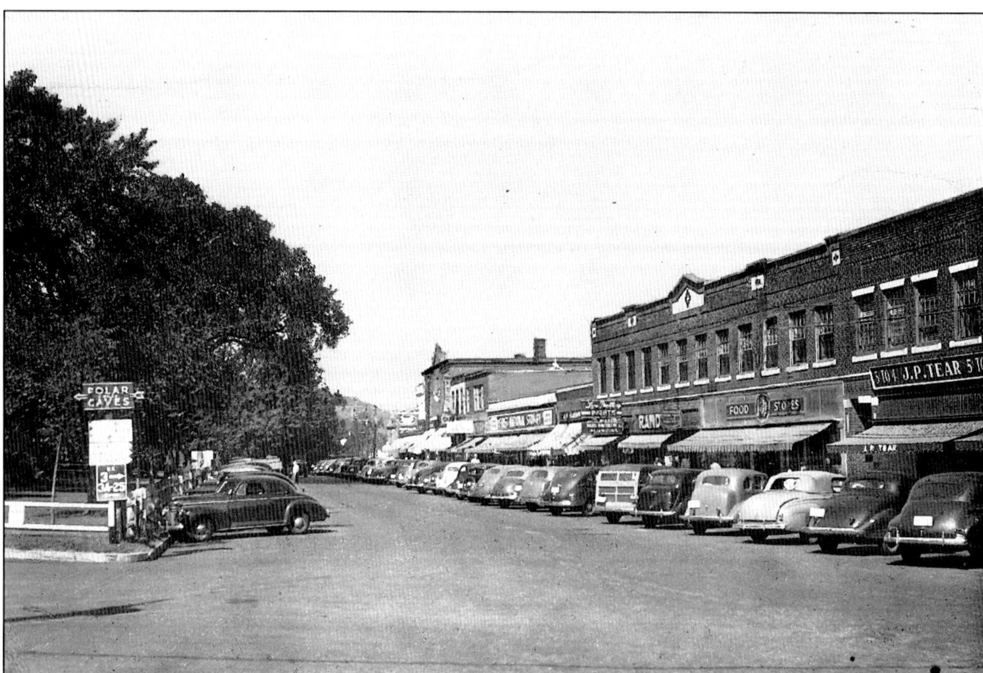

Between the 1870s and the 1940s, quite a few changes had taken place on Main Street.

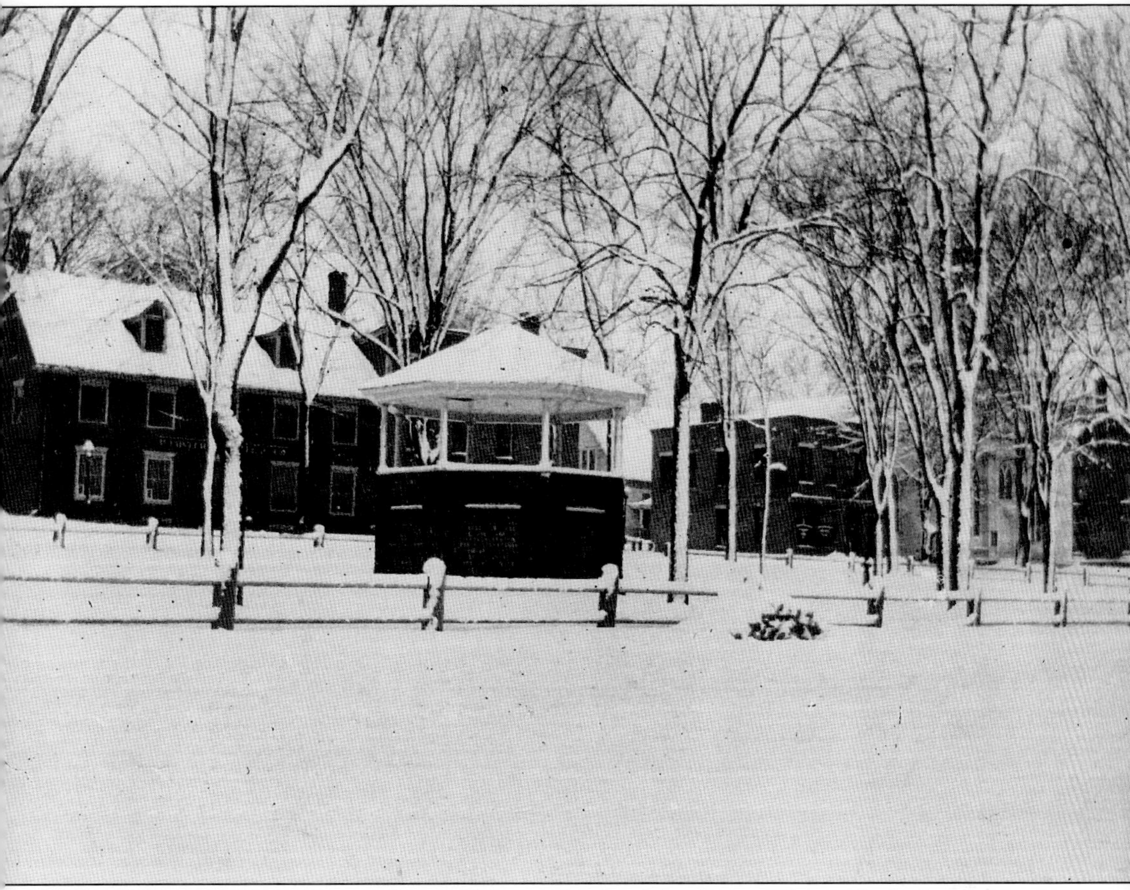

The Bullfinch bandstand, erected in 1903, was designed by the grandson of noted architect Charles Bullfinch, also the nephew of Mrs. Plummer Fox of Plymouth. It still serves as the center of summer concerts, which were originated by John Keniston in 1902.

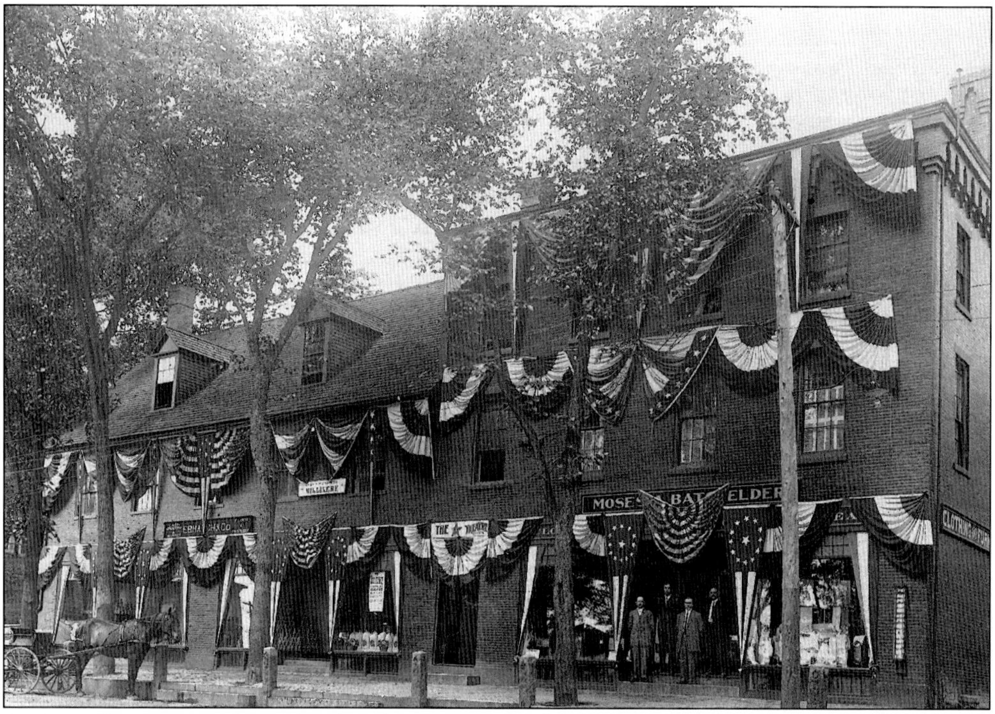

Built on the corner of Highland and Main Streets by Moor Russell in 1822, "the Old Brick" housed a variety of business establishments before being razed in 1936 to make way for the present post office.

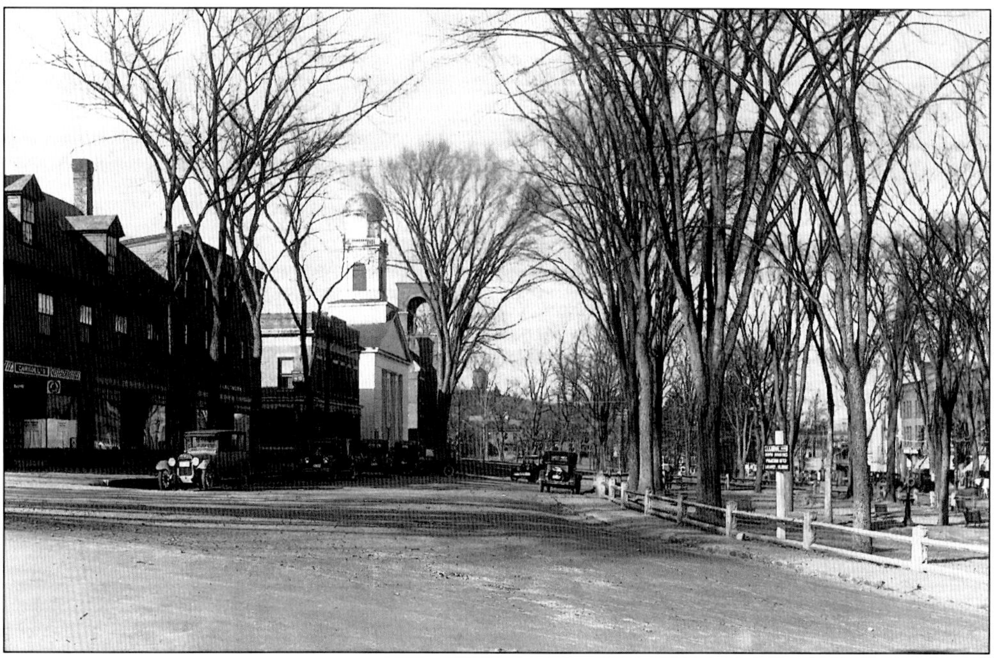

This view of the Common in the 1930s shows some of the stately elm trees which shaded local streets for many years. The car at the top of the Common was not going in the wrong direction; rotary traffic would not be adopted for another ten years or so.

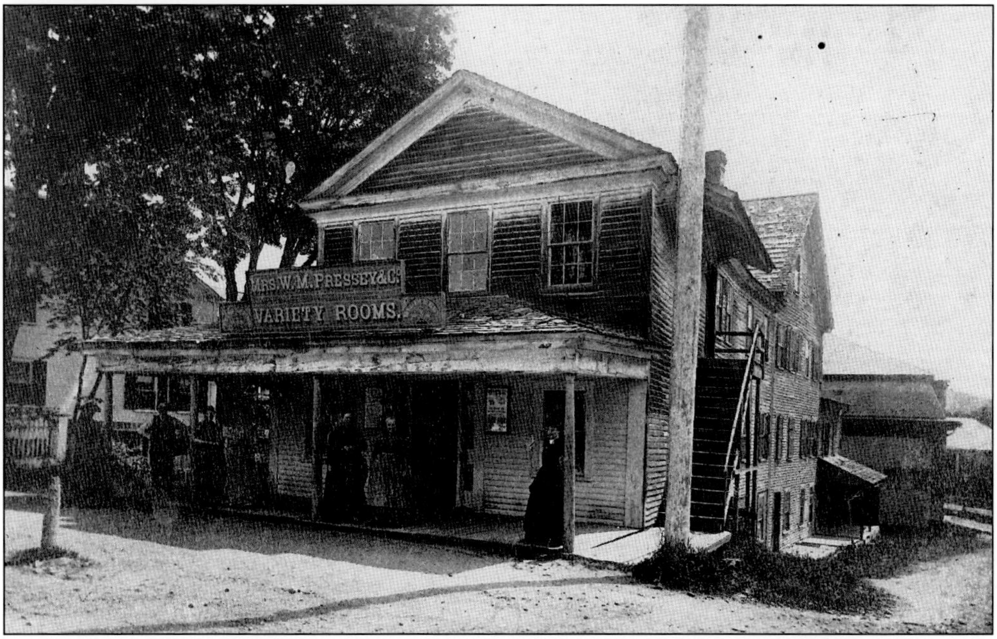

Mrs. Warren Pressey kept a millinery shop for several years where Volpe's now is in the Rollins Block . . .

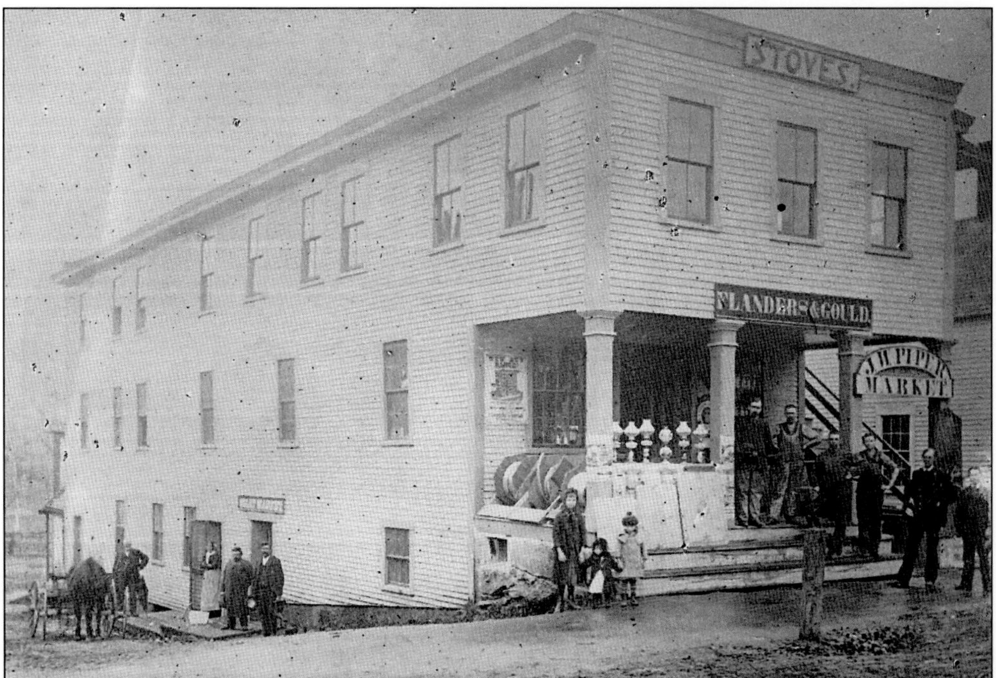

. . . and the Flanders & Gould plumbing business, often called the Tin Shop, became in later years the Blake Building.

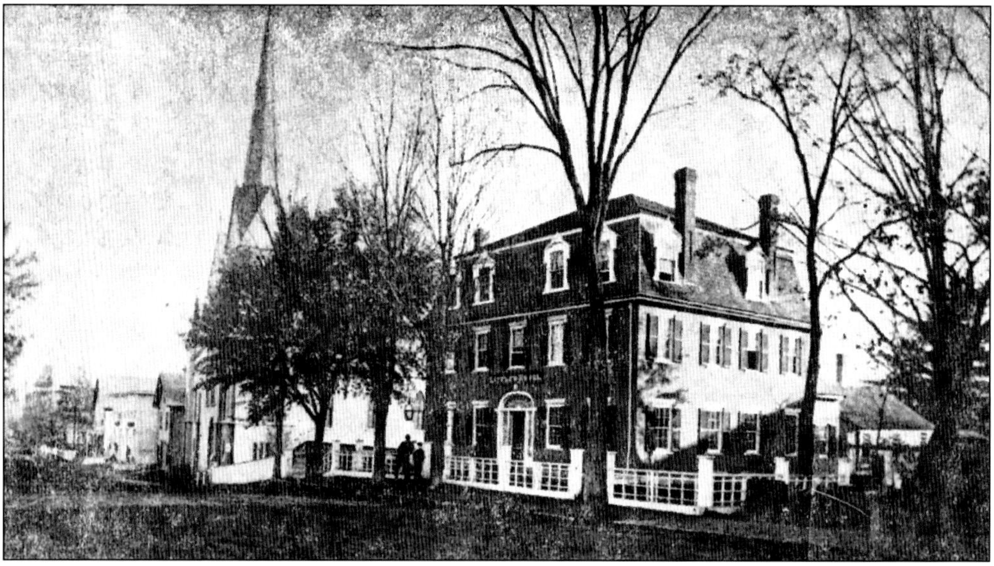

The Thompson Building, which became Little's Hotel, was razed in 1888 for construction of the Kidder Block.

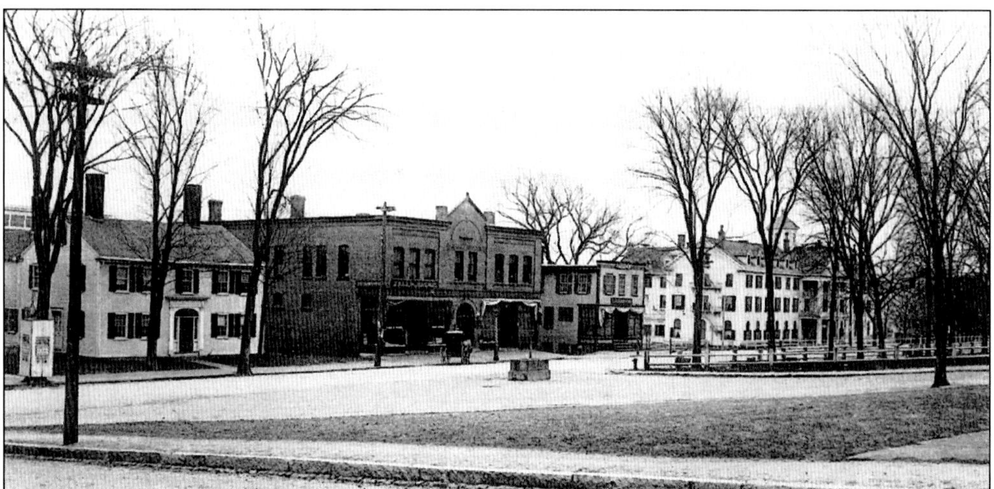

Although the Howe house (left) and the second Pemigewasset Hotel (right) both succumbed to fire, the Rollins Block, erected in 1893 and twice badly damaged by fire, remains one of the oldest buildings on Main Street.

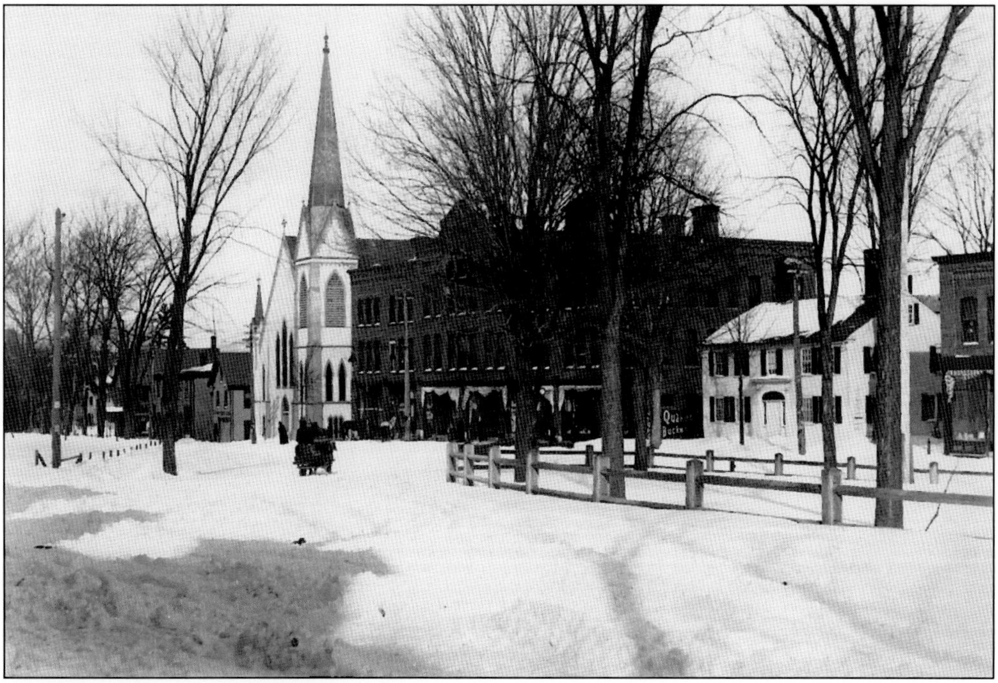

The Methodist church and the Kidder Block, both destroyed by fire in 1943, and the Howe house, burned in 1935, together presented an impressive facade at the north end of the Common.

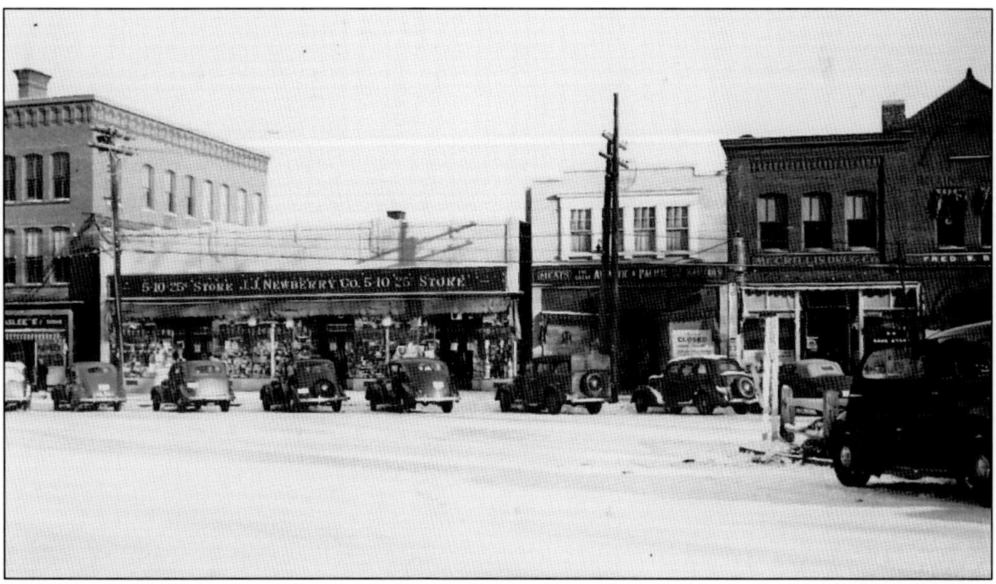

The fire and subsequent razing of the Howe house in 1935 made way for J.J. Newberry and the A&P market. The A&P soon moved to a larger space in the Rand block farther south on Main Street, and Newberry's expanded into the A&P's space.

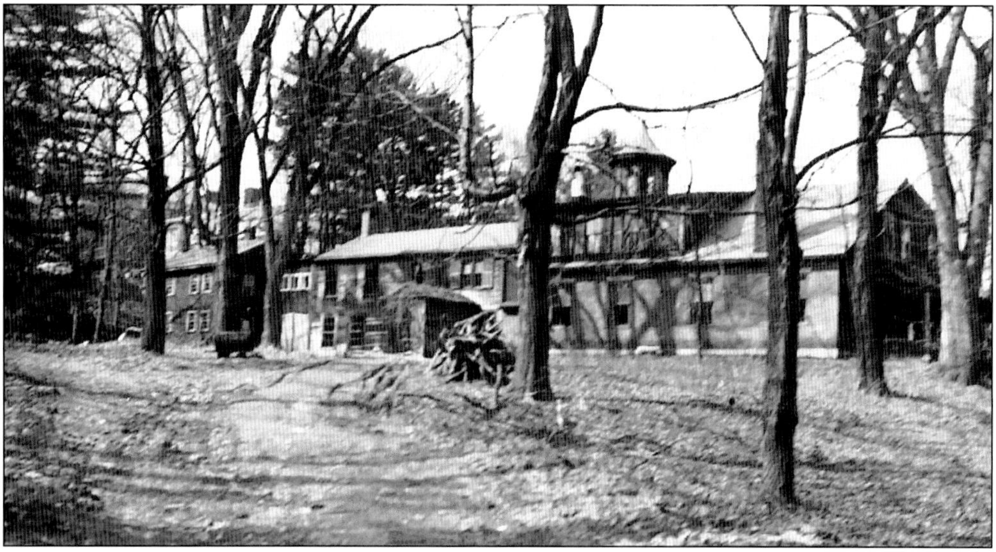

Attorney Nathaniel Rogers built his elegant mansion in 1825, and it soon became a center of hospitality. Hosting the poet John Greenleaf Whittier among others, Mr. Rogers, a strong abolitionist, entertained many national advocates of freedom. The home contained a secret room in which runaway slaves were hidden during their flight north to Canada on the Underground Railroad.

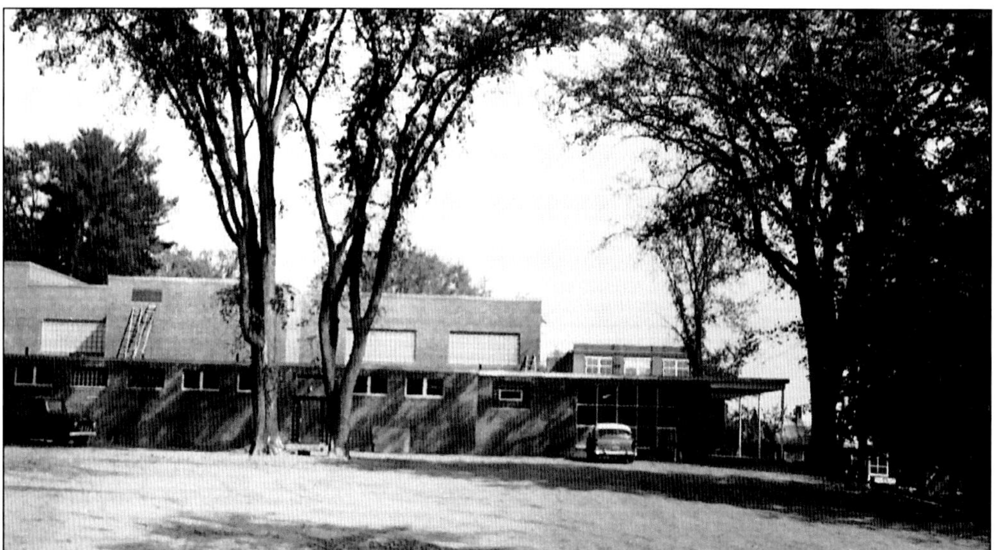

The Rogers home was razed in 1954 for the building of Silver Hall by Plymouth State College. It was later remodeled and enlarged as the present-day Silver Cultural Arts Center, which offers the area a wide variety of plays, concerts, and other events.

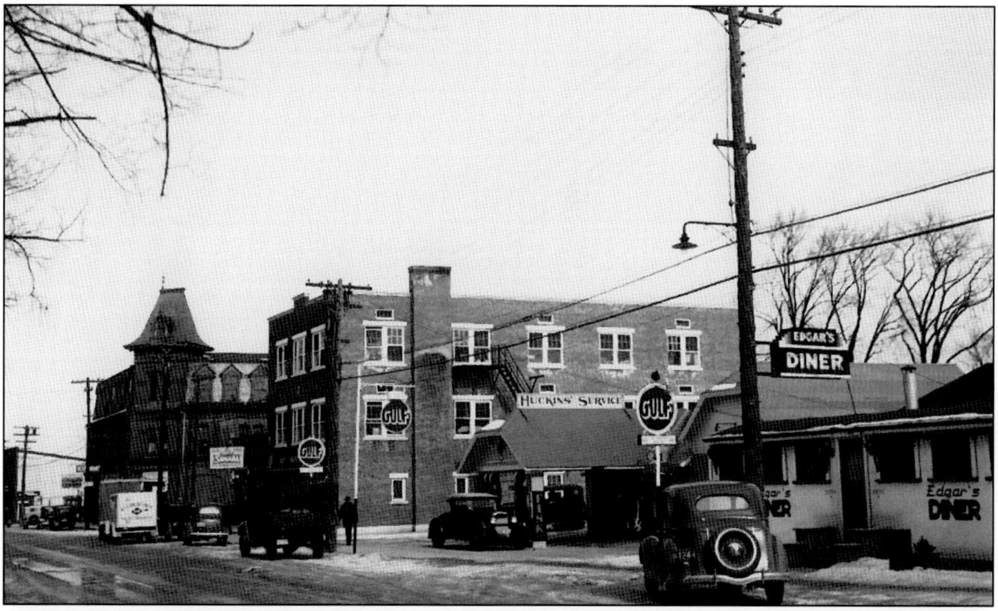

Edgar's Diner, Huckin's Gulf Station, and the Sargent Block are no longer the familiar landmarks they once were on Main Street, but Samaha's store and the Harry Ronan Building still remain—the former still operated by the family of Norman Samaha and the latter having undergone several transitions through the years.

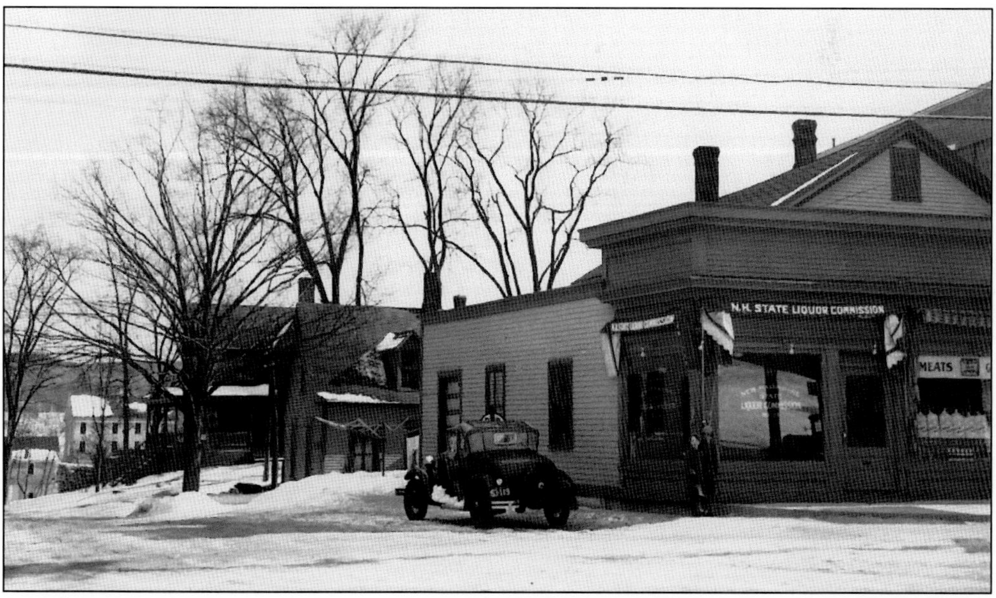

Samaha's grocery store, at the corner of Main and Bridge Streets, was opened in 1917 by Louis Samaha, who came here from Syria in 1910 to join his brother Abdelnour. The oldest established grocery business in Plymouth is now operated by the third generation of the family.

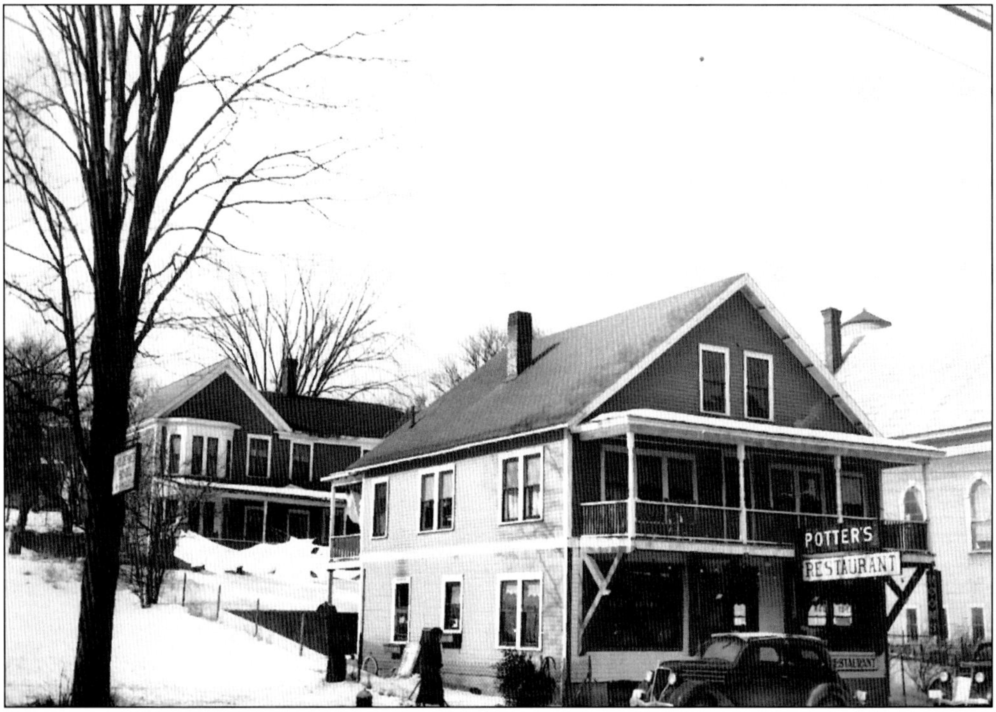

In 1930, Edward "Scottie" Potter arrived from Liverpool, England, and opened a small restaurant at the north corner of High and Main Streets. He enlarged it to the building shown here and operated it with Mrs. Potter for many years. They gained a well-deserved reputation for their meals and hospitality.

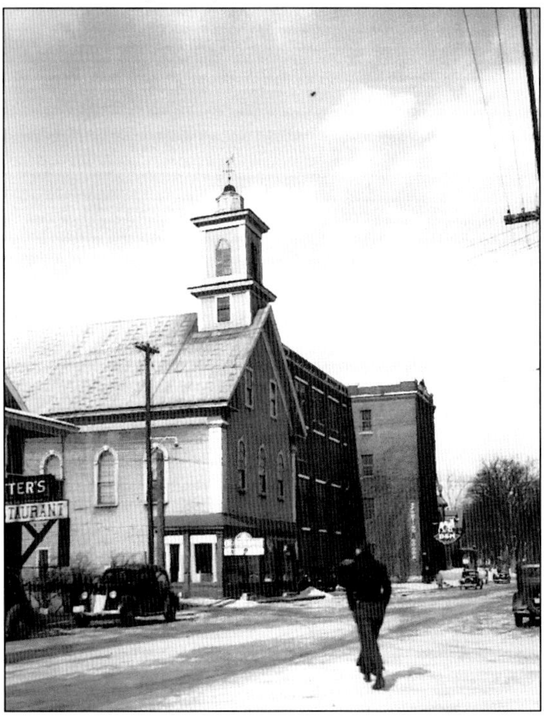
Cook's Hall, on the north corner of High and Main Streets, began as the Congregational church in Campton at Wishman Corner. Built in 1802, it served as a church until 1858, was unoccupied for several years, and was sold to G.W. Keniston in 1864. Dismantled and bought by Freeman Cook, it was brought to Plymouth, re-erected over a new first floor, and served as the town hall until it was razed in 1938 for the widening of High Street.

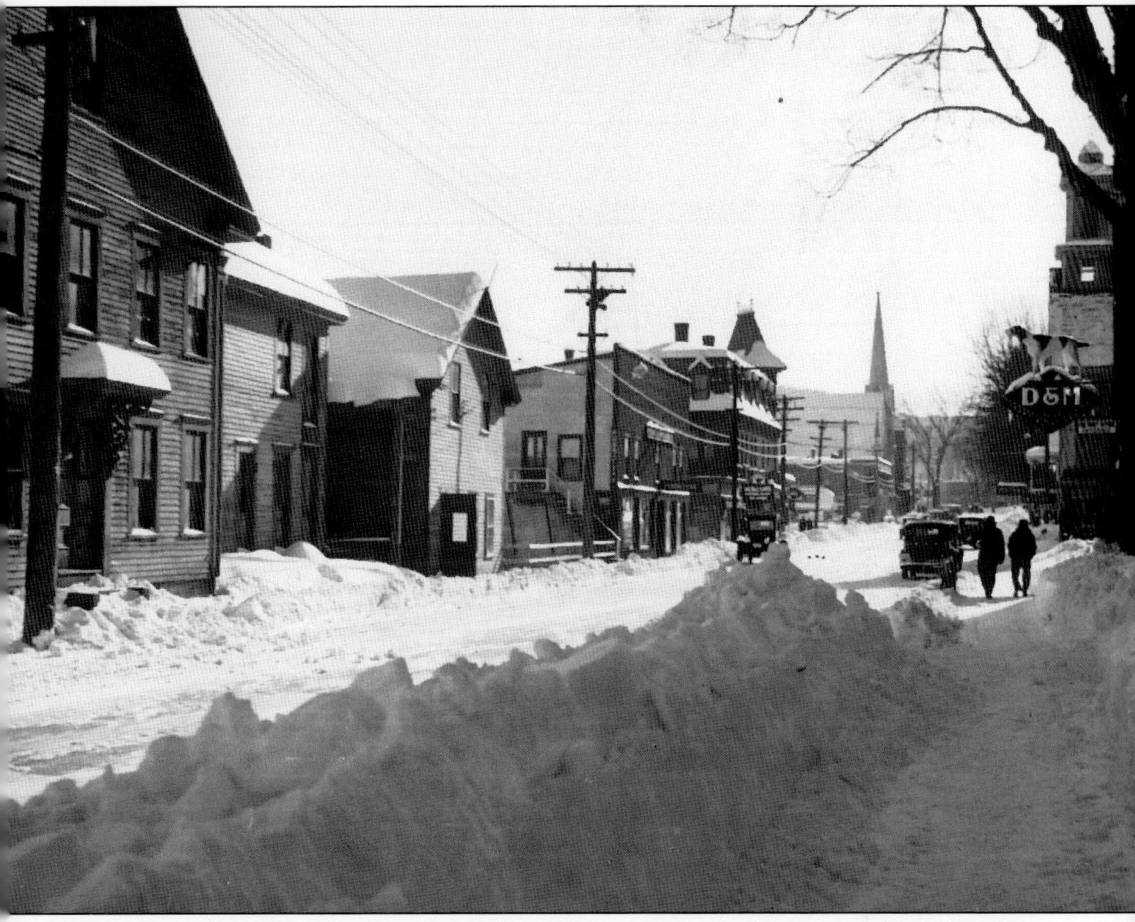

Perhaps the only building now recognizable on the east side of Main Street, north of Bridge Street, is the Steinman building, home of Plymouth Furniture Company. At least one of the other buildings shown here is one of the "Ten-Footers" moved to this location from opposite the Common.

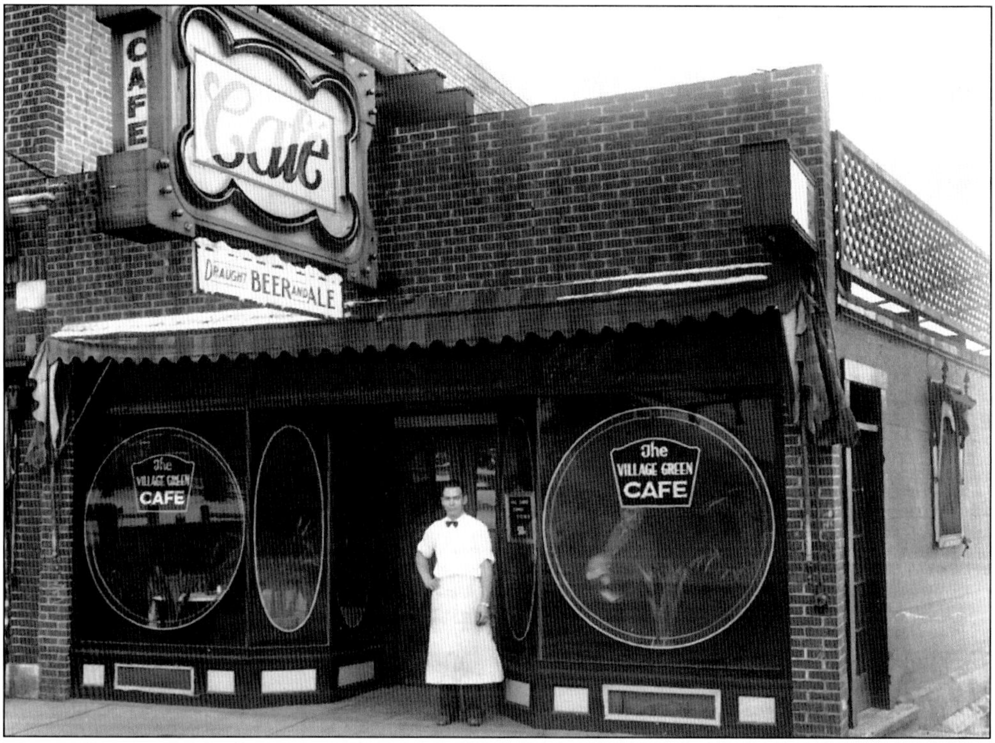

The Village Green Cafe, now Anderson's Bakery, was a fixture on Main Street for many years. Leo Ouellette Sr. stands ready for customers next to a sign offering "full course dinner specials—50 cents."

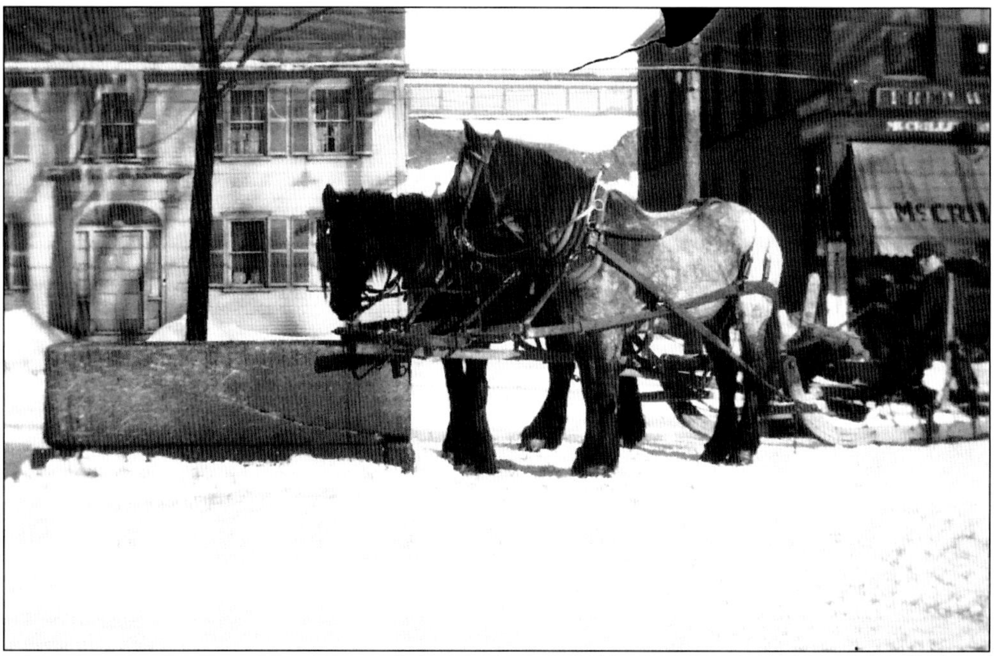

The watering trough at the north end of the Common was a welcome stop for horses around the turn of the century. It now is at Crystal Spring, south of the town.

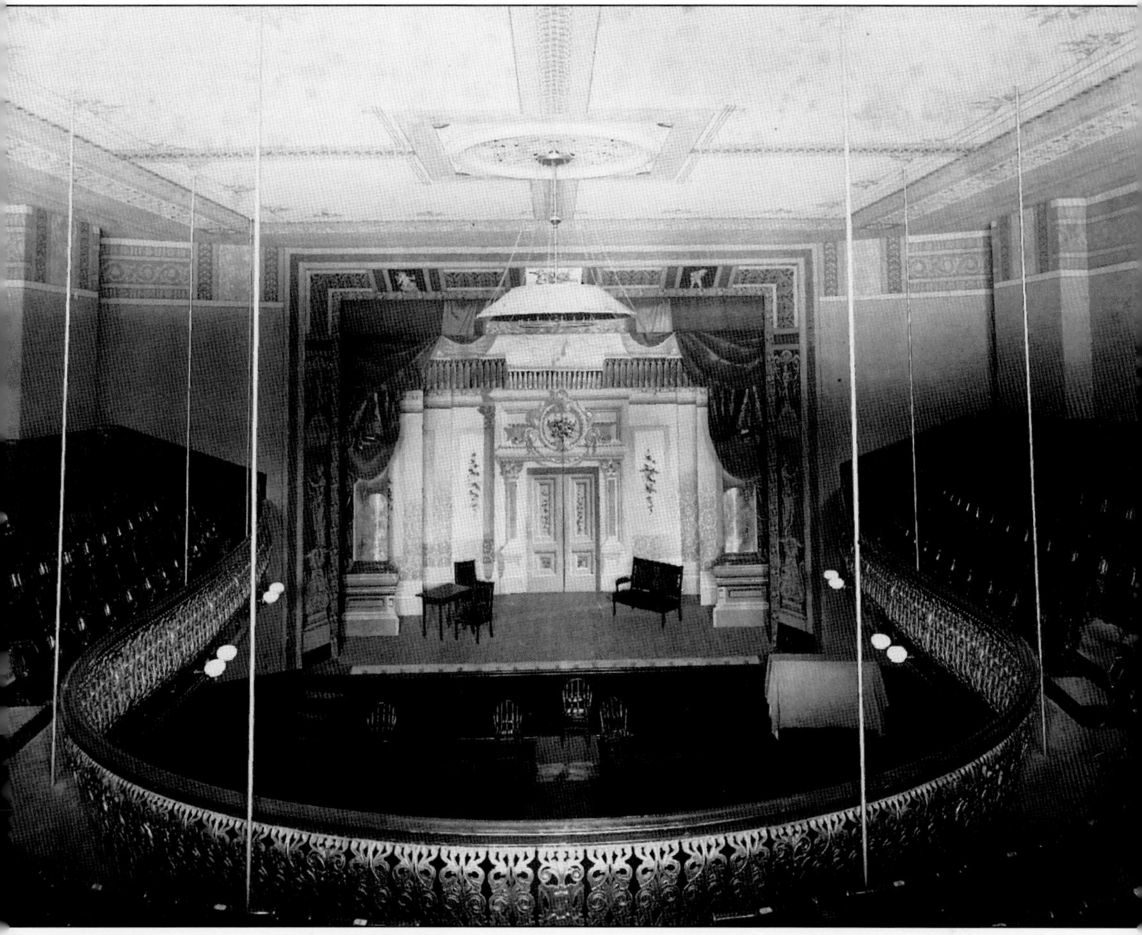

The spacious theater in the Kidder Block was the scene of musical and dramatic presentations as well as lectures and town meetings. It was sorely missed by the community after the fire of 1943.

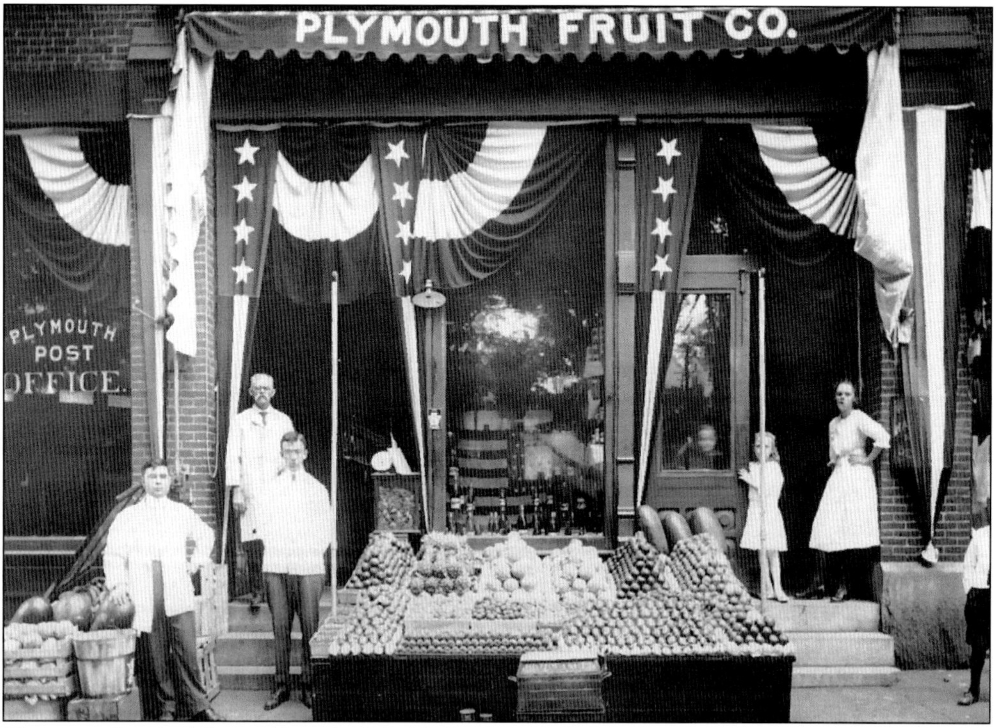

The street level of the Kidder Block held the post office and Joe Albany's fruit market, proudly decked out for the sesquicentennial celebration in 1913.

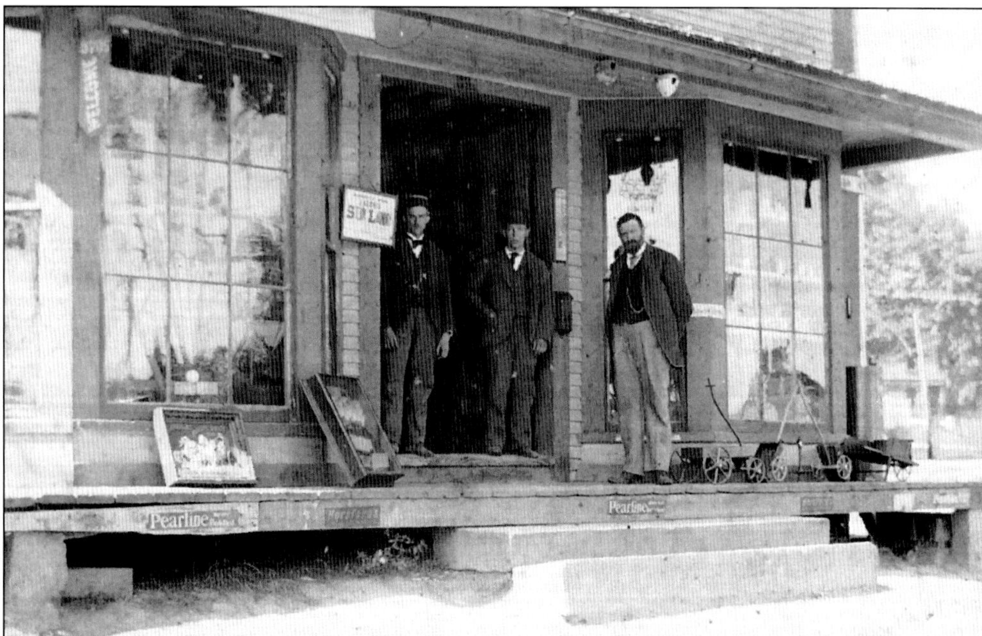

Holding an informal business discussion on the porch of the Plummer Fox Store in the early 1890s were Frank Fox, Fred Corliss, and Plummer Fox. The Plummer Fox Store was the first of three Fox buildings to occupy this location.

Two

Tourism and the Railroad

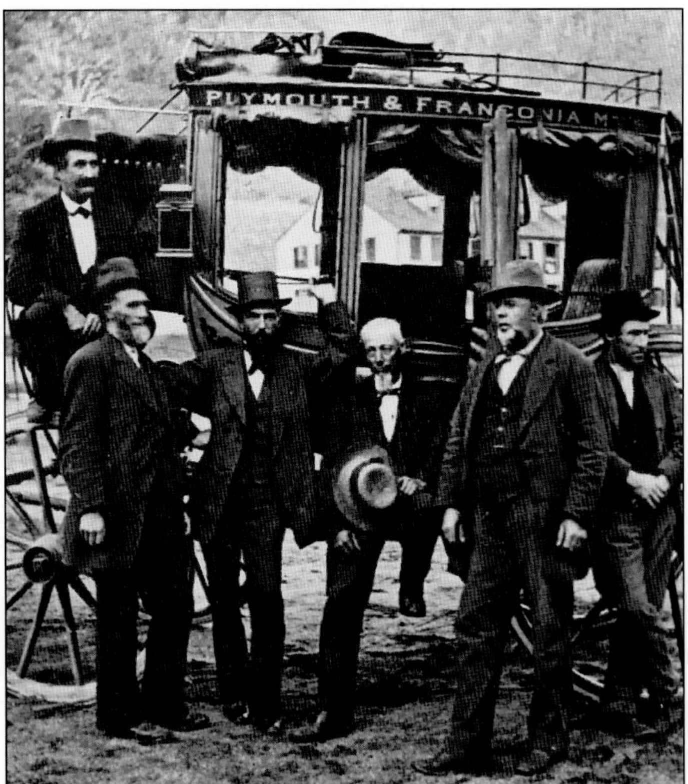

Nestled in the foothills of the White Mountains, Plymouth has long been a starting place for tourists on their journey through New Hampshire's mountain beauty. This early photograph of the PLYMOUTH-FRANCONIA stagecoach depicts early transportation up the Pemigewasset Valley through the "Notch" to Franconia. Drivers for the stagecoach were a hardy group and several of them made their homes in Plymouth. After the railroad came to Plymouth bringing summer visitors, the stagecoach business to the north was brisk indeed.

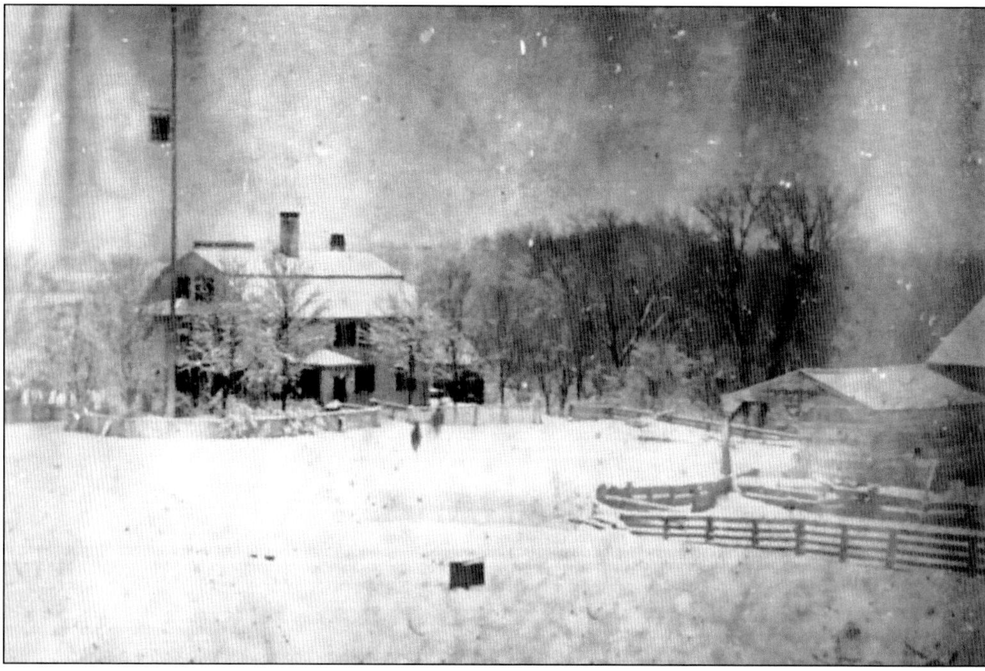

Col. David Webster built a small log tavern in 1764 which was later replaced by a small framed house. This was enlarged as business increased. His son, William Webster, later built a gambrel-roofed building which he ran as a tavern for judges and other court officials. The rude structure is said to be part of the first log tavern.

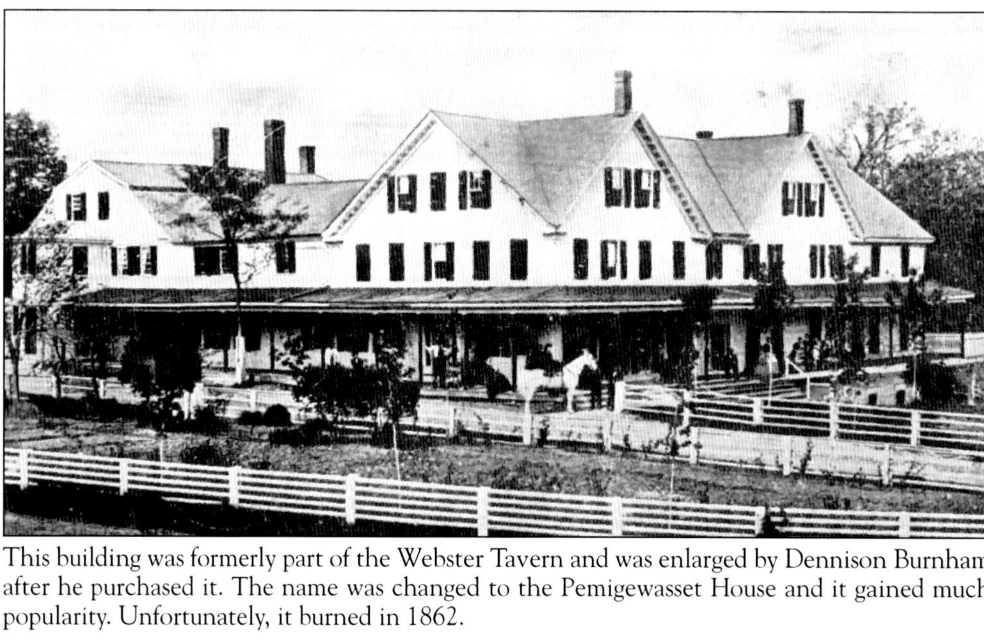

This building was formerly part of the Webster Tavern and was enlarged by Dennison Burnham after he purchased it. The name was changed to the Pemigewasset House and it gained much popularity. Unfortunately, it burned in 1862.

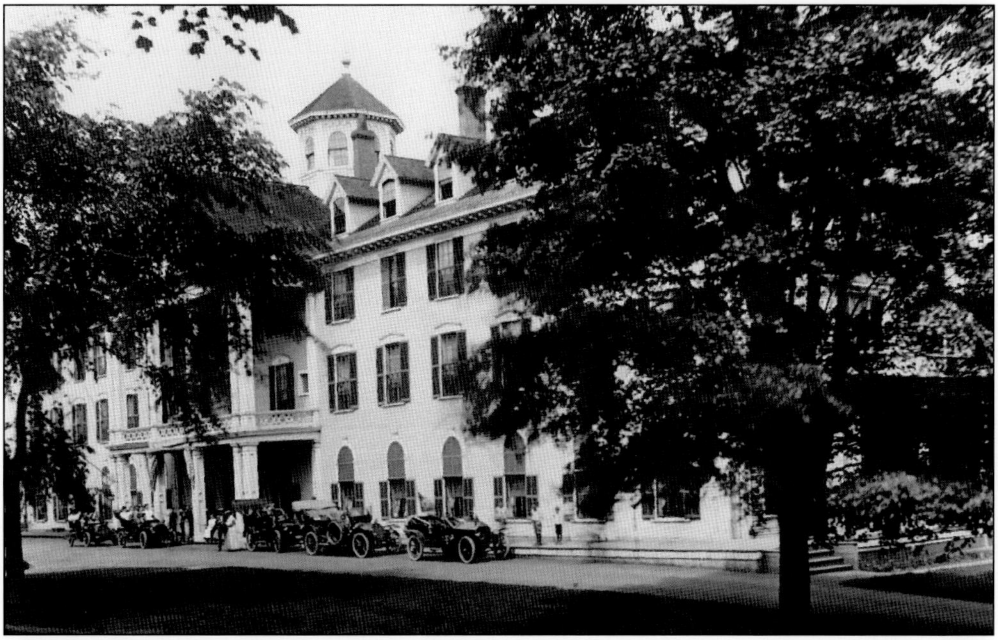

This elegant hotel was built to replace the first Pemigewasset House. It was located on Main Street and was a prominent feature of the town. The railroad trains stopped for meals at the lower level of the hotel. Until it was destroyed by fire in 1909, the hotel made a fine combination with the railroad. Many well-known people lodged here, including Nathaniel Hawthorne. In poor health and accompanied by his friend, former U.S. President Franklin Pierce, Hawthorne came to the hotel to recuperate, but died here on May 19, 1864.

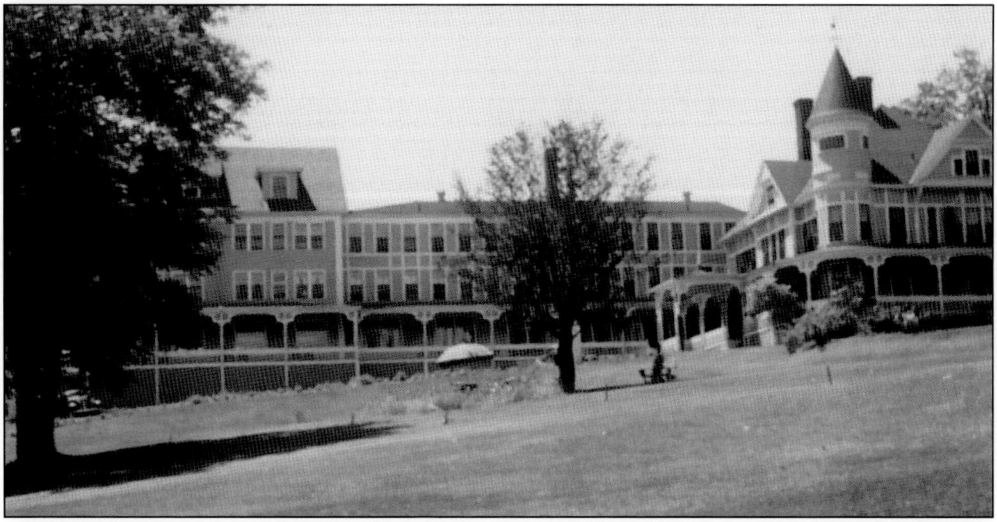

This popular hotel was made from the home of Amos M. Kidder (on the right) and what was formerly the Plymouth Normal School dormitory. Large windows on the north side gave guests and diners magnificent views of the mountains up the Pemigewasset Valley. From 1912 to 1958, the year it was damaged by a severe fire, the Pemigewasset Hotel enjoyed a brisk business, as tourism was a large part of Plymouth's livelihood. After the fire, the State purchased the property for Plymouth State College. Presently Pemigewasset Hall and the Lamson Library occupy the site.

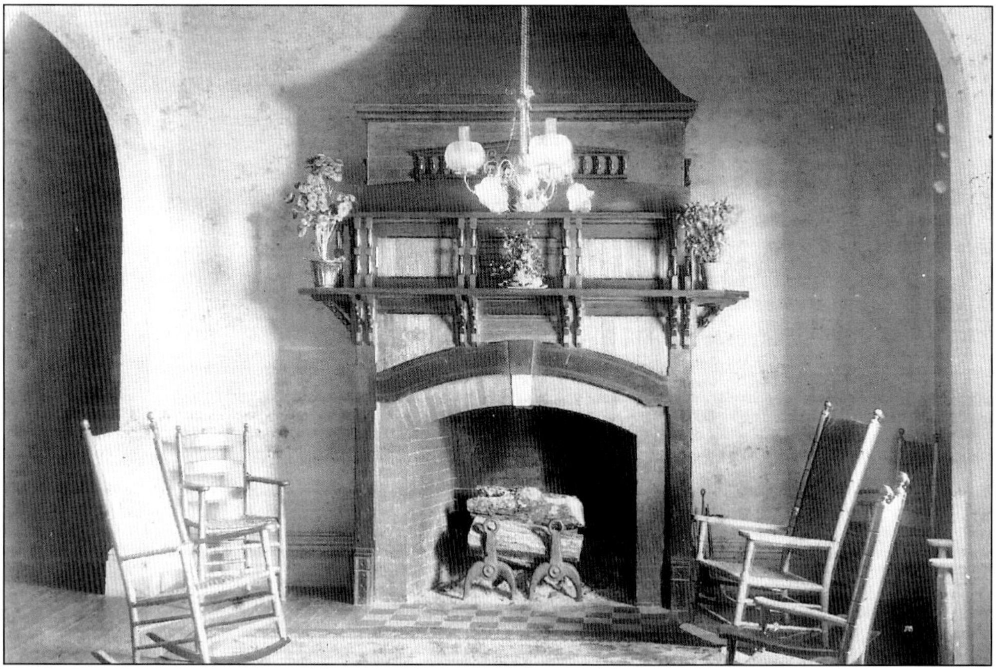

In the days of the large downtown Pemigewasset Hotel, which also served as Plymouth's railroad station, these rocking chairs by the fireplace awaited weary travelers. Taking note of the arched doorways, one can imagine that the Pemi was built on a large scale with many fine features; the design of the fireplace also suggests this.

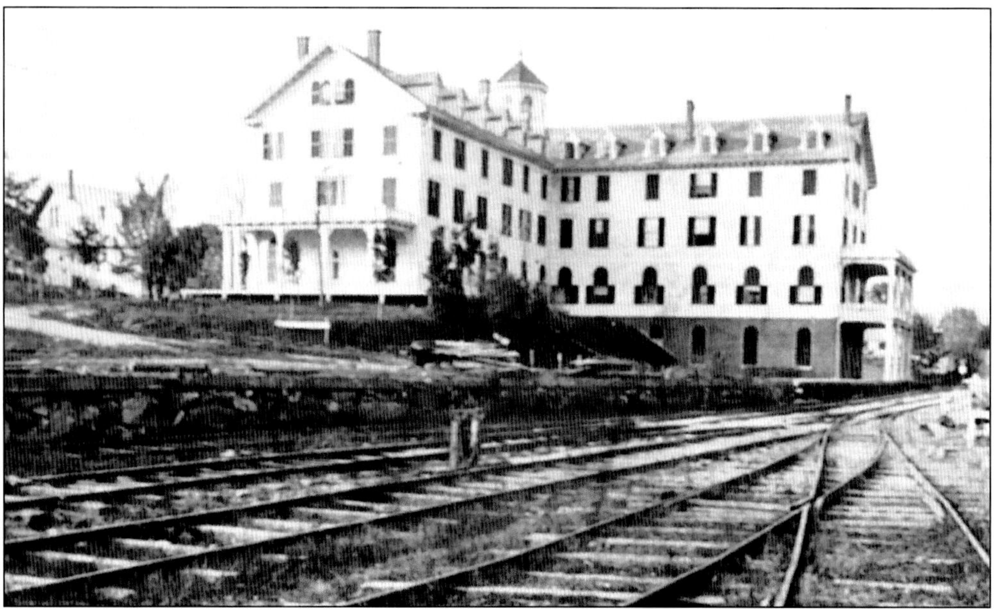

After the first Pemigewasset House was destroyed by fire, Mr. John E. Lyons, manager of the railroad, realized that the growing volume of summer traffic required hotel accommodations. Accordingly, the railroad financed the building of a fine, split-level hotel. A single-story extension on the ground level provided the station and restaurant with access to the fine dining room in the hotel above. Many trains stopped here for food and fuel.

Daily at noon and again at 5:00 p.m., trains arrived in Plymouth from both the north and south. Passengers would leave the train and eat in either the station restaurant or the dining room upstairs in the Pemigewasset House. This menu gives an idea of the extensive selection offered to patrons of the dining room. Watching the trains arrive and observing the passengers' fashions were high entertainment for many in the town.

PEMIGEWASSET HOUSE,

PLYMOUTH, N. H. - - - C. H. MARDEN, Manager.

Menu.

Little Neck Clams.

Cream of Celery. Consomme with Rice.

Fresh Salmon with Green Peas. Baked Bluefish, Wine Sauce.
Potatoes Chateau. Iced Cucumbers. Queen Olives.

Fowl and Pork, Cream Sauce. Beef Tongue.

Fillet de Bœuf aux Champignons.
Spaghuetti a l' Italienne.
Rice Croquettes with Jelly.
Chicken a la Creole.

Damson Plum Sherbet.

Rib of Beef, Dish Gravy. Turkey, Cranberry Sauce.
Spring Lamb, Green Mint Sauce. Gosling, Apple Sauce.

Lobster en Mayonnaise. Kalamazoo Celery. Potato Salad.

New Potatoes, boiled and mashed. Bermuda Onions.
New Beets. Native Green Peas. Boiled Rice.
Marrow Squash. Beet Greens. Corn.

Baked Indian Pudding with Cream. Snow Pudding.
Apple Pie. Currant Pie. Cream Pie. Angel Cake.
Sunshine Cake. Swiss Cake.

Strawberry Ice Cream.

Charlotte Russe. Cream Puffs. Claret Jelly. Lemon Jelly.
Biscuit Glace. Layer Raisins.
Figs. Assorted Nuts. Watermelon.
Strawberries and Cream.

Edam Cheese. American Cheese. Pineapple Cheese.

Tea. Coffee.

SUNDAY, JULY 15, 1888.

THE NAME "PEMIGEWASSET" HAS BEEN CONNECTED WITH A HOTEL IN PLYMOUTH SINCE THE REVOLUTION PERIOD, AND MOTORISTS OF TO-DAY HAVE COME TO KNOW OF ITS CHARM, COMFORT AND CUISINE AS DID THE PASSENGER ON THE OLD STAGE COACHES

RATES

ARE DECIDEDLY IN KEEPING WITH THE TIMES AND ARE ON THE AMERICAN PLAN

$5, $6 & $7 PER DAY PER PERSON

SPECIAL WEEKLY RATES ON APPLICATION

ALL ROOMS ARE WITH BATH OR RUNNING HOT AND COLD WATER

TABLE D'HOTE MEALS

BREAKFAST $1.25
LUNCHEON $1.50
DINNER $1.75

PLYMOUTH HAS A VERY SPORTY

NINE HOLE GOLF COURSE

AVAILABLE FOR THE USE OF OUR GUESTS ON PAYMENT OF THE MODERATE DAILY GREENS FEE OF $1.50 PER DAY
$2 FOR SUNDAYS AND HOLIDAYS
$7.50 PER WEEK, OR $15 FOR 20 DAYS PLAY

GOOD BATHING AND FISHING

ARE ENJOYED AT BOTH ASQUAM LAKE, 8 MILES AWAY, OR NEWFOUND LAKE, WHERE BASS, SALMON AND LAKE TROUT ABOUND IN SEASON

DISTANCES FROM PLYMOUTH.

BOSTON	126	LAKE SUNAPPE	60
MANCHESTER	69	GREENFIELD	140
CONCORD	50	NEW YORK	340
GORHAM	100	WHITEFIELD	55
BRETTON WOODS	50		
COLEBROOK	120		
FRANCONIA NOTCH	32		
CRAWFORD NOTCH	55		

PLYMOUTH

NEW HAMPSHIRE

AT THE GATEWAY TO THE WHITE MOUNTAINS

THE

PEMIGEWASSET

W. F. ADAMS, LESSEE
E. C. WRIGHT, MANAGER

PLYMOUTH'S

LEADING HOTEL

This hotel brochure promotes the area as a popular resort, and the rates make one wish for "the good old days." The reverse side notes that parents of children at the numerous summer camps in the area will find convenient accommodations at the "Pemi."

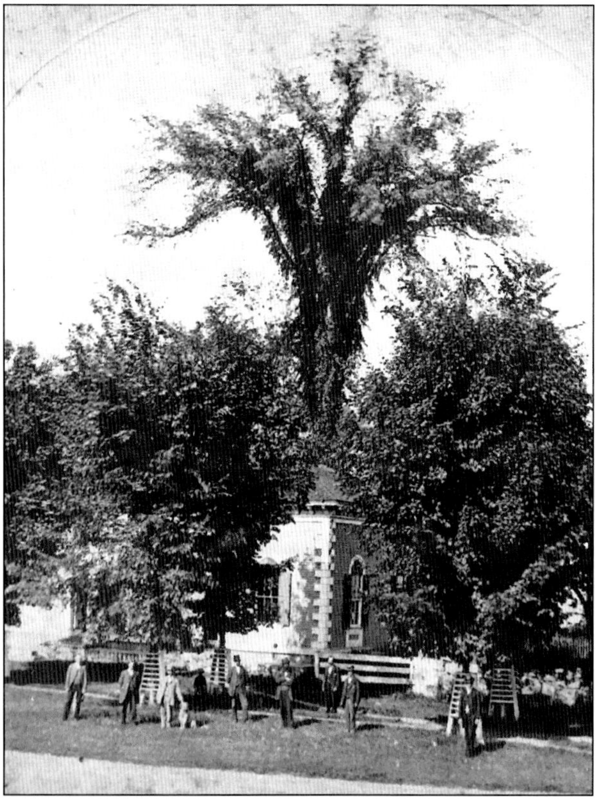

Josiah Quincy, a local lawyer, was the first president of the Boston, Concord & Montreal Railroad corporation. For many years its main office was located in this handsome building in Railroad Square with the Starr King Elm in the background. The arrival of the first train in Plymouth began a new era for the area. Tracks were soon extended to Woodsville with service to Littleton via the Connecticut River Valley. This expansion not only benefited local merchants, but created a growing need for more hotels, guest houses, and cabin colonies for the increasing numbers of "summer boarders." The Plymouth tourist industry was born!

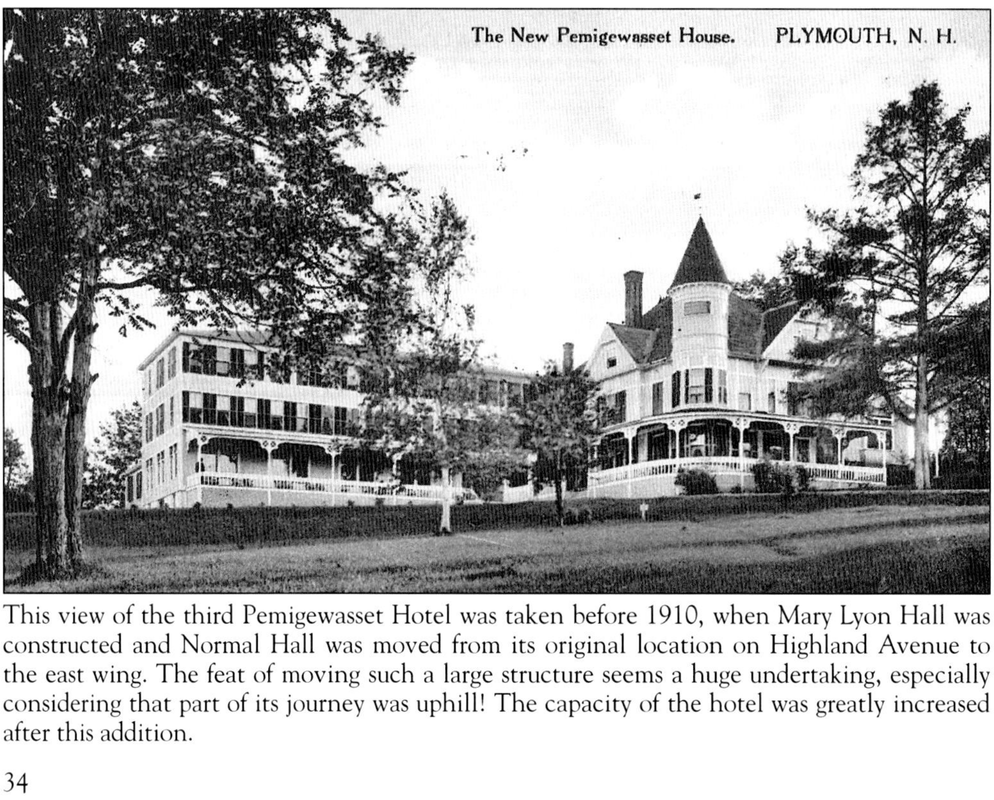

This view of the third Pemigewasset Hotel was taken before 1910, when Mary Lyon Hall was constructed and Normal Hall was moved from its original location on Highland Avenue to the east wing. The feat of moving such a large structure seems a huge undertaking, especially considering that part of its journey was uphill! The capacity of the hotel was greatly increased after this addition.

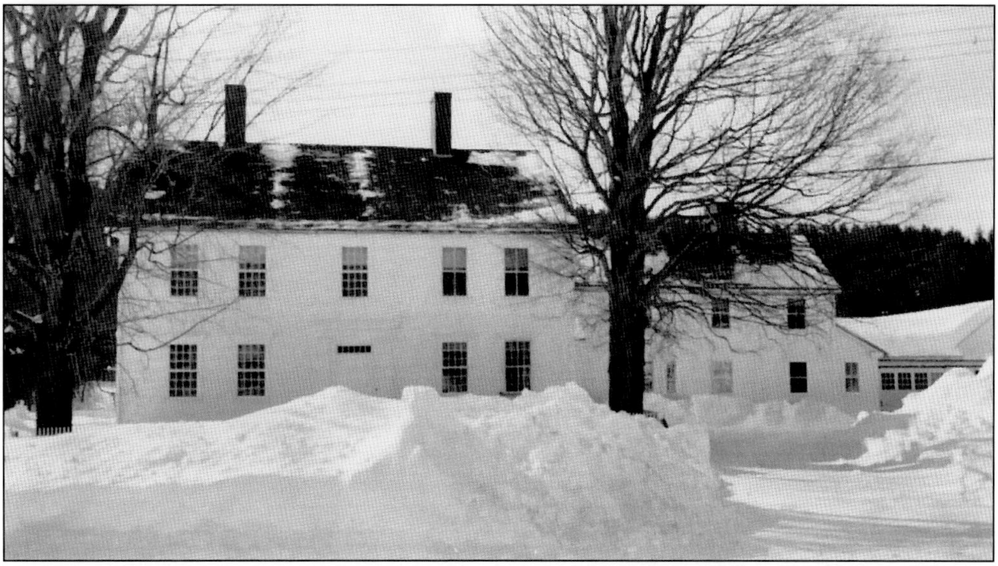

"Clarkland," long the home of local benefactor George G. Clark, was built in 1800 by Samuel Wells as a tavern and inn. Originally, there was no ell and the kitchen occupied the northwest corner. The entire front of the second floor was a dance hall, and the Masonic order of Plymouth was organized here in 1803. During its ownership by the Clark family, the farm became a showplace of the Baker River Valley. It currently houses the Harris Family Furniture business.

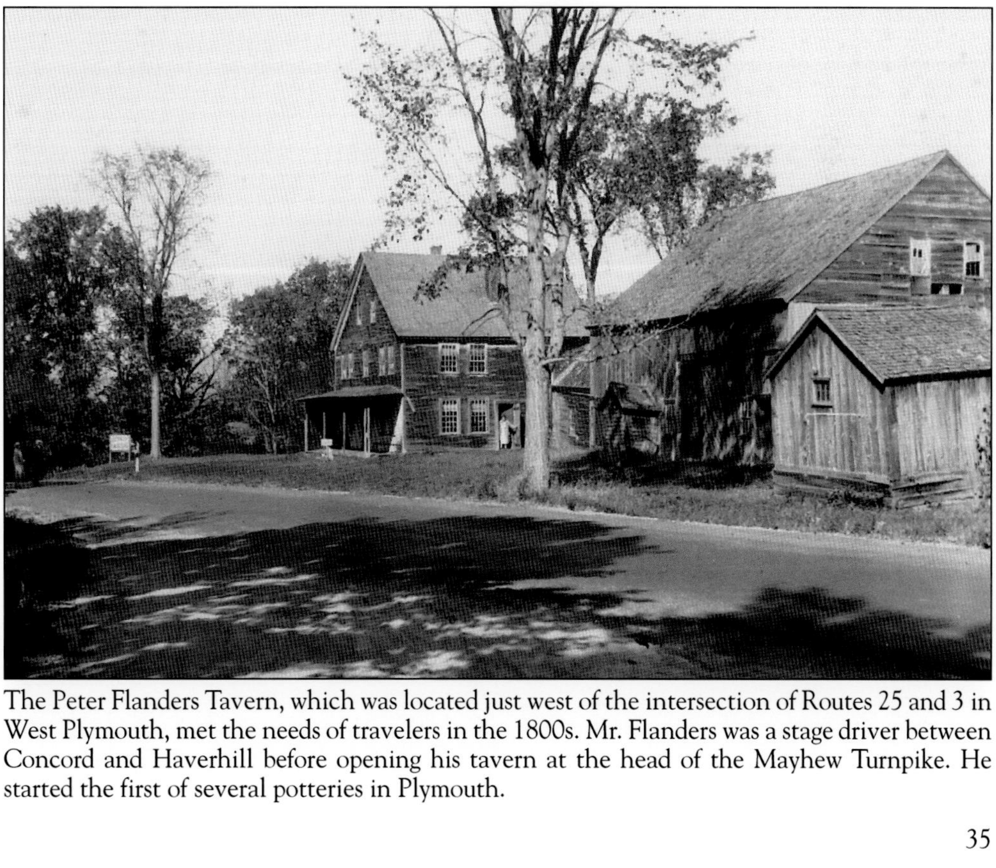

The Peter Flanders Tavern, which was located just west of the intersection of Routes 25 and 3 in West Plymouth, met the needs of travelers in the 1800s. Mr. Flanders was a stage driver between Concord and Haverhill before opening his tavern at the head of the Mayhew Turnpike. He started the first of several potteries in Plymouth.

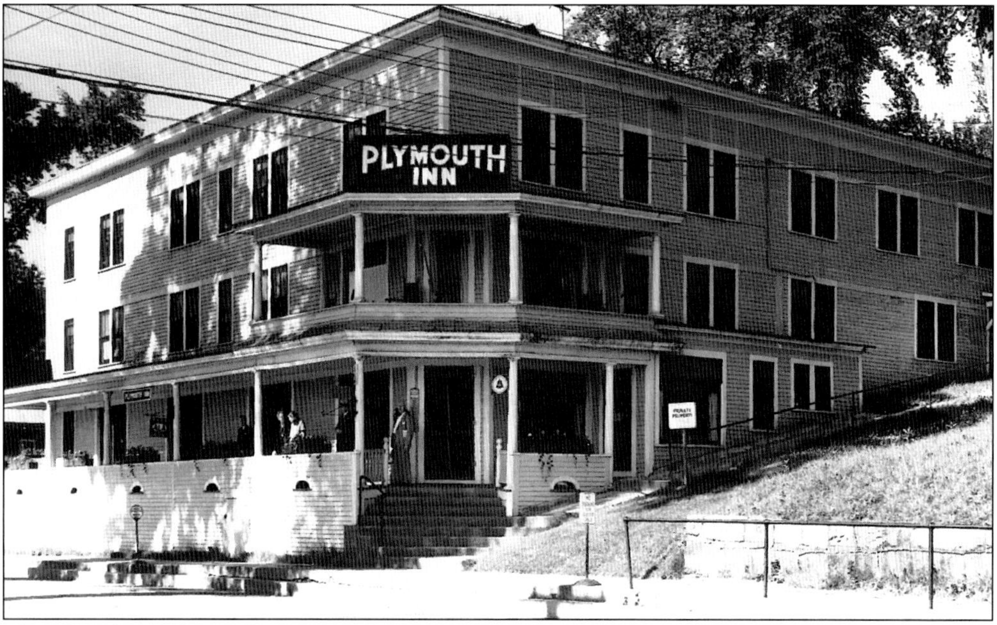

This fine hotel located on Main Street was run by the Arthur Carpenter family for over 50 years. It was known for its hearty, delicious meals and warm hospitality. It was a popular accommodation for the many skiers who came to Plymouth on the Snow Trains.

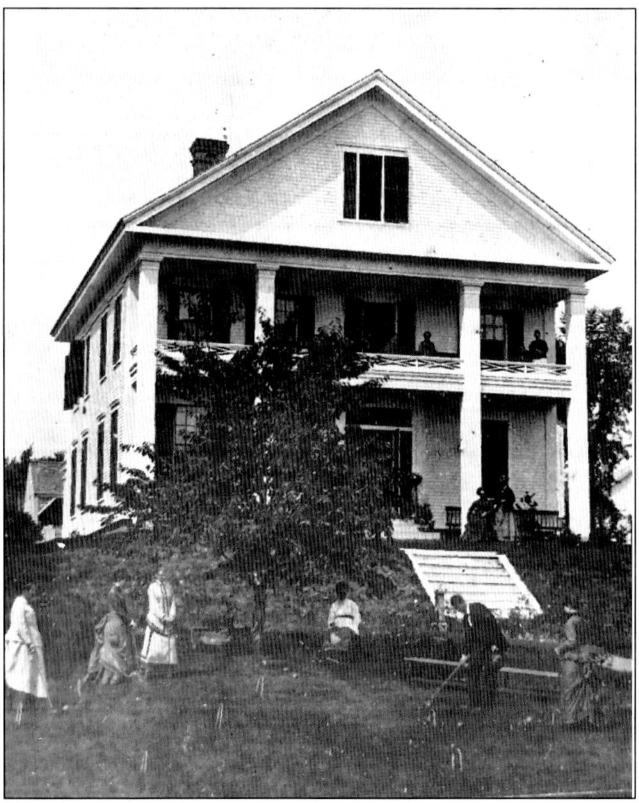

Roselawn, a lovely two-story, pillared home overlooking Main Street, was built by a grandson of Col. David Webster in 1854. It was so named because of a lovely rose garden on the grounds. The garden was enjoyed by passersby and guests of the Pemi House across Main Street. It was later opened as a guest house and today is an apartment complex.

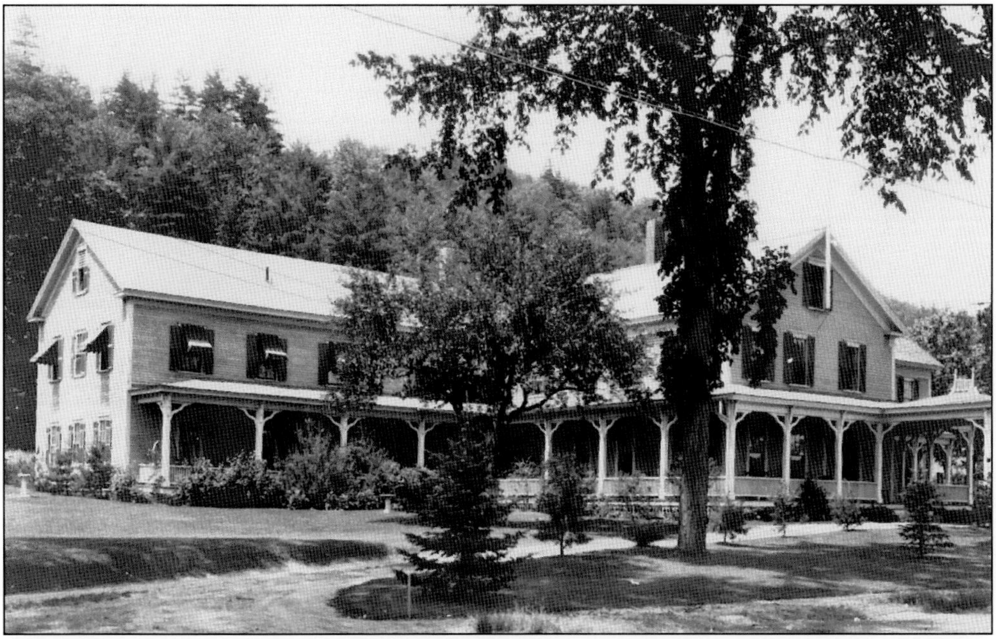

Originally a hops farm owned by David Webster, this attractive structure on Route 3 north of Plymouth village had various additions over the years in its life as an inn. It has been known as Elmwood, Western Slopes Lodge, and Mount Prospect Lodge. It is today occupied by the Wreath School.

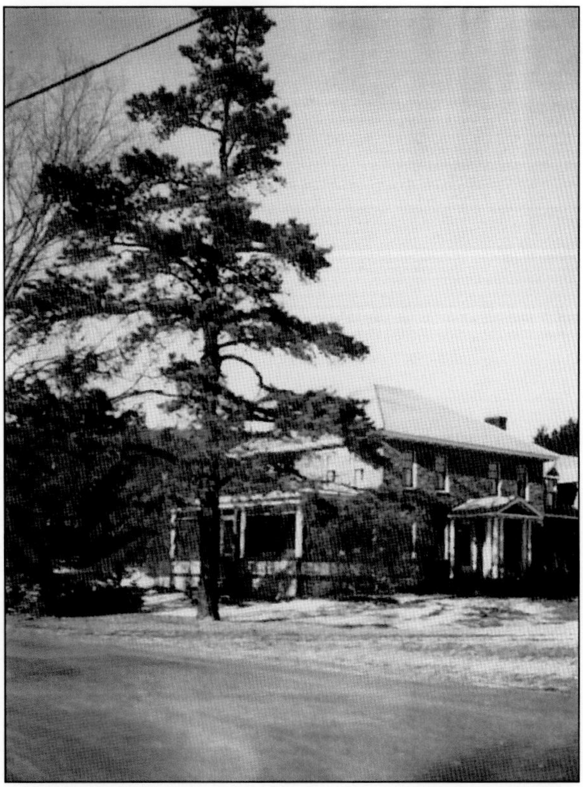

Tobey's Motel was a pioneer in the new trend of connected units rather than separated cabins. It was one of the oldest motels east of the Mississippi. Many of the Tobey units had kitchenettes and garages, and its dining room was a well-known place to dine. Following a fire which destroyed many of the motel units, the main building has been used as a nursing home and is currently an office complex.

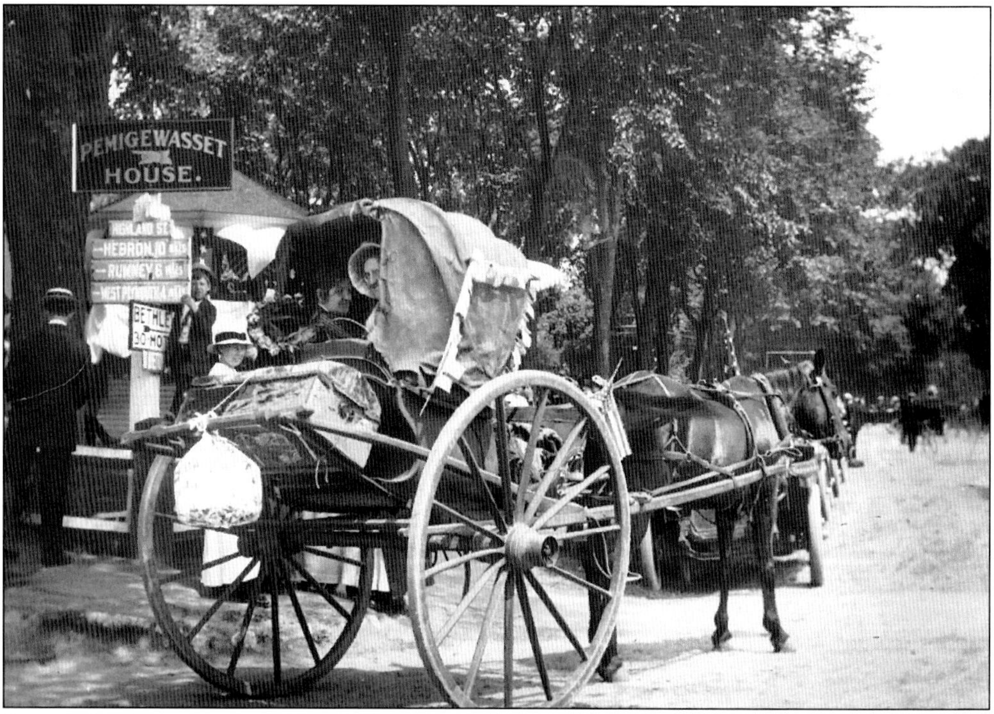

During the festivities connected with Plymouth's 150th birthday celebration in 1913, Dr. John Rogers's shay was driven about town. In this photograph it can be seen near the sign post at the south end of the Common which is topped by a good-sized sign pointing the way up Highland Street to the Pemigewasset Hotel. Distances to nearby towns are also given.

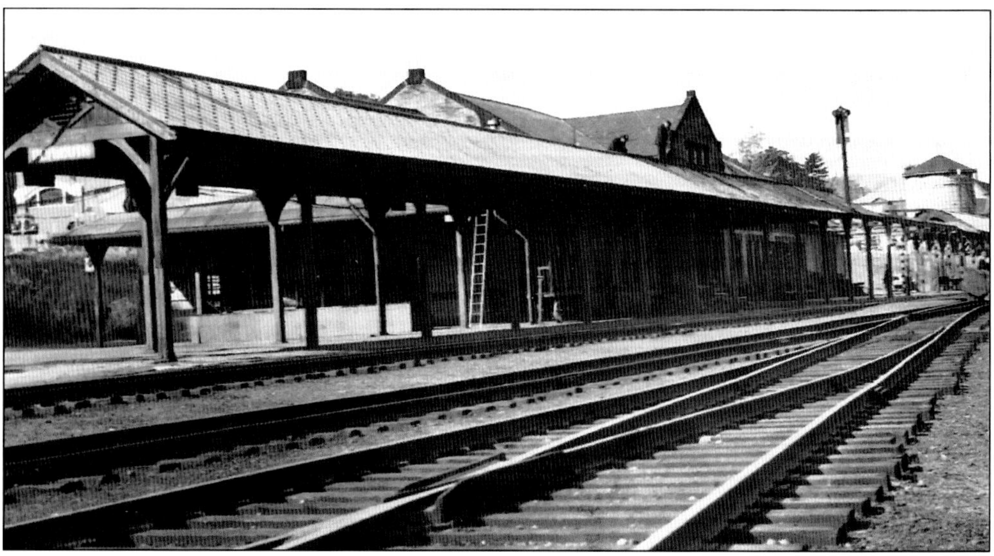

This view of the railroad station looking north shows many of the tracks, the canopy covering the platform, and the water tower in the distance.

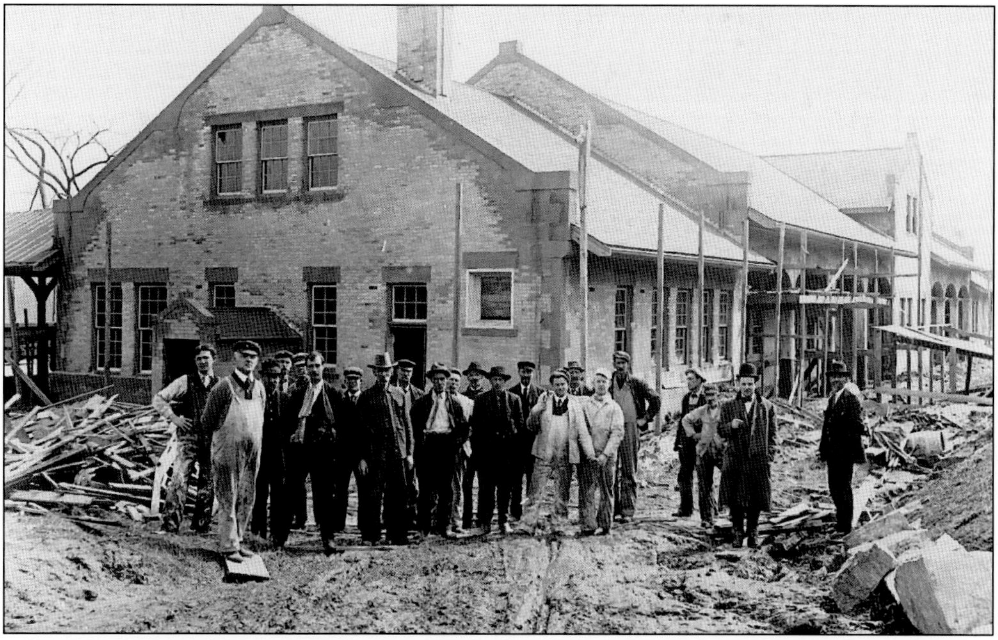

After the Pemigewasset Hotel was destroyed by the disastrous fire in 1909, a fine brick structure was planned by the railroad to serve as a passenger station with a dining room and freight facilities. Constructed of two colors of brick and built right next to the tracks, it was used by the railroad daily until the end of passenger service in 1959.

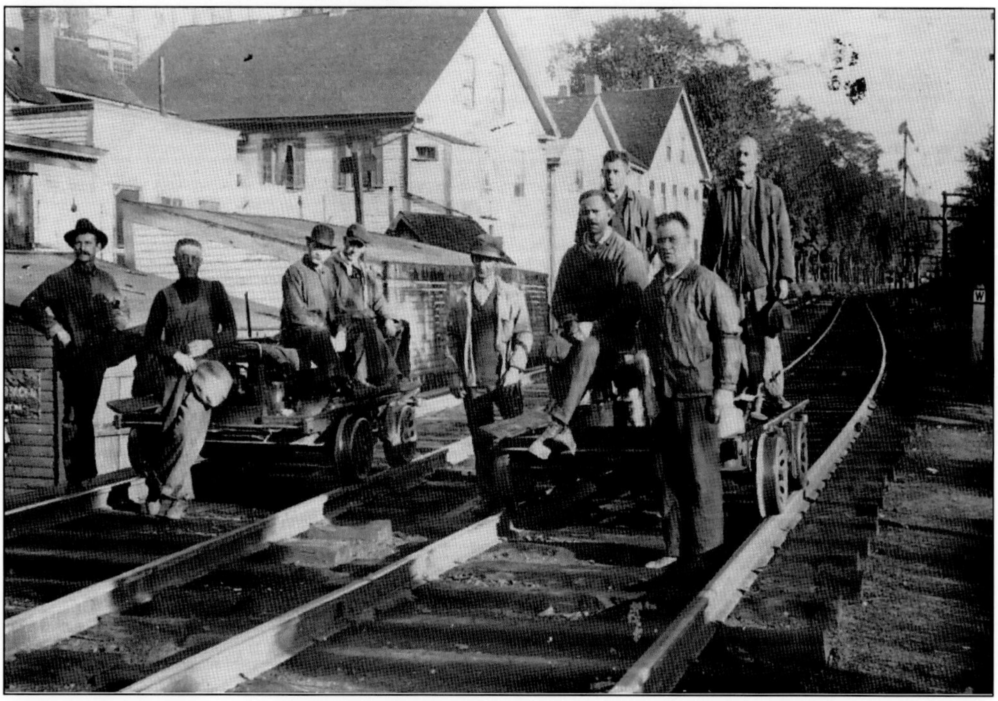

Keeping the tracks and roadbeds smooth and in good repair was a never-ending job for the section crew. This crew was photographed just north of the crossing on Bridge Street. The wood frame buildings were on North Main Street opposite the D&M factory.

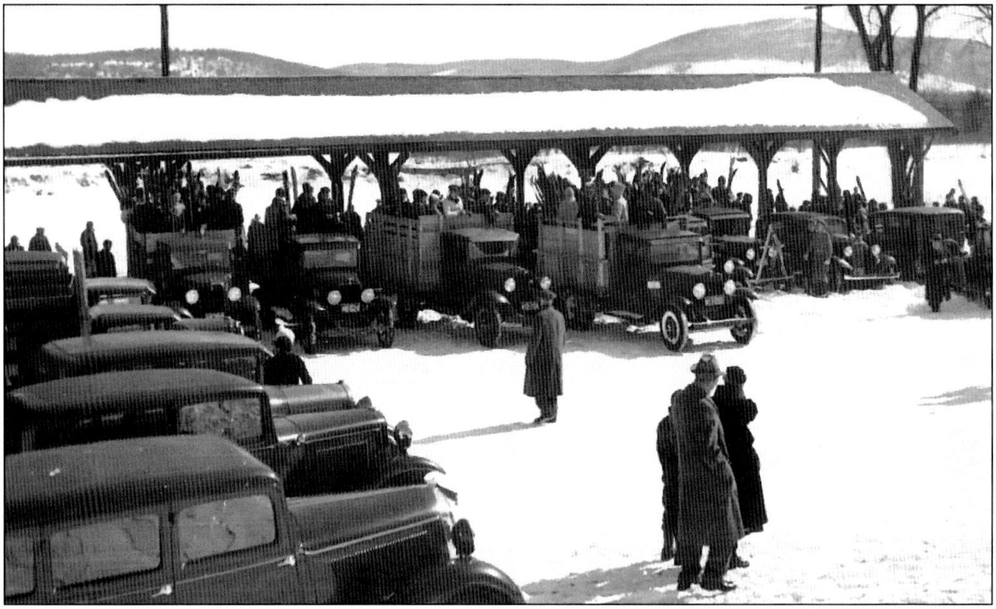

In the winters of the 1930s and until World War II, the Plymouth railroad station was a beehive of activity on weekends. "Snow Trains" brought hundreds of skiers to Plymouth. From the station, they walked or were driven to the many fine accommodations in the area and then enjoyed the several ski areas nearby. There were ski tows at Frontenac (just off Parker Street), at Wendy's (off Route 3 just south of town), and at Huckins Hill across the river in Holderness. The more energetic skiers were driven to Tenny Hill, where they hiked to the top for a run down the mountain. For a brief period Plymouth was indeed a major ski resort in the East.

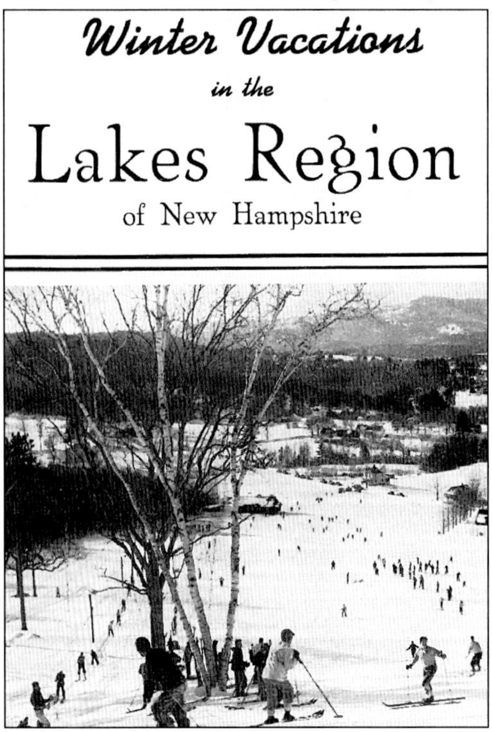

In the 1930s and into the 1950s, this popular slope, located just off the south side of Parker Street, offered pleasant skiing for those interested in the rapidly growing sport. Frontenac, as it was called, provided a rope tow to transport skiers up the hill with relative ease for only a modest fee. For the less adventurous skier, getting off the tow at the "birches" was the usual procedure. In the Swiss-style chalet at the base of the hill, satisfying snacks and hot drinks awaited the hungry skiers. This hill adjoined "Wendy's" Ski Slope on the other side of Walker Hill. It was just off Route 3, so both areas were within comfortable walking distance from the downtown hotels. The ski train enthusiasts, as well as local persons, took full advantage of the slopes.

Three

INDUSTRY

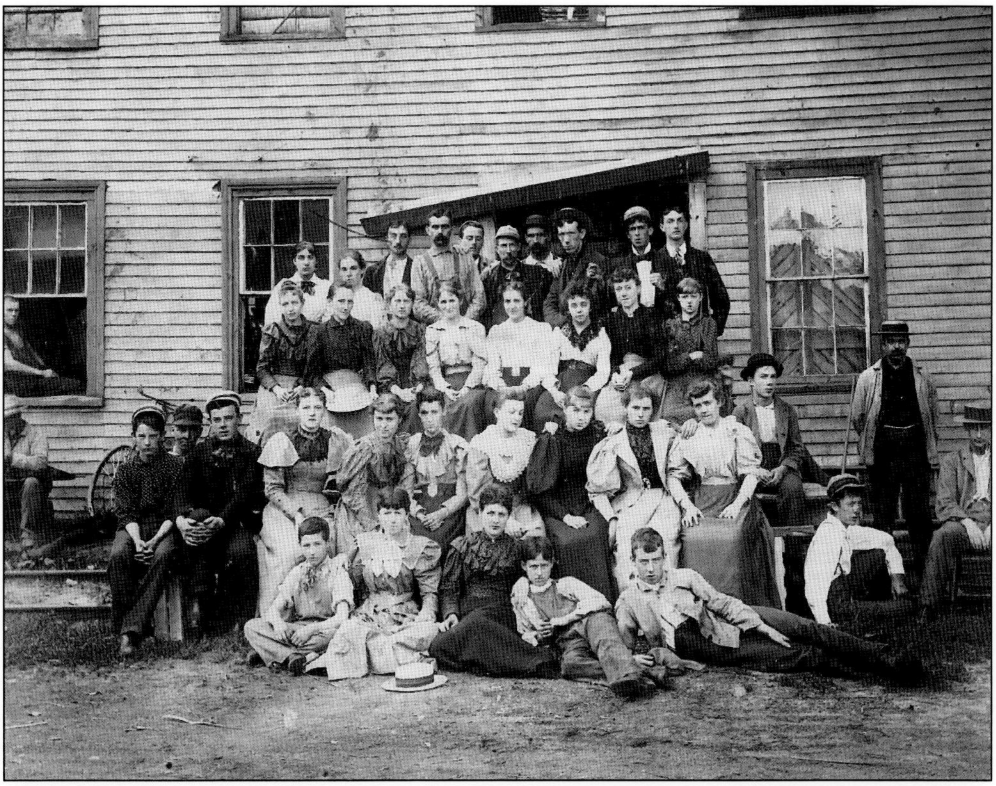

The Peg Mill was built in 1898 by Edmund J. and George R. Foster, two brothers from Shelburne Falls, Massachusetts. The mill brought employment to many people during its tenure. Owners of the plant have continued to offer such opportunity through the years even to this day in its capacity as the Plymouth Manufacturing Company.

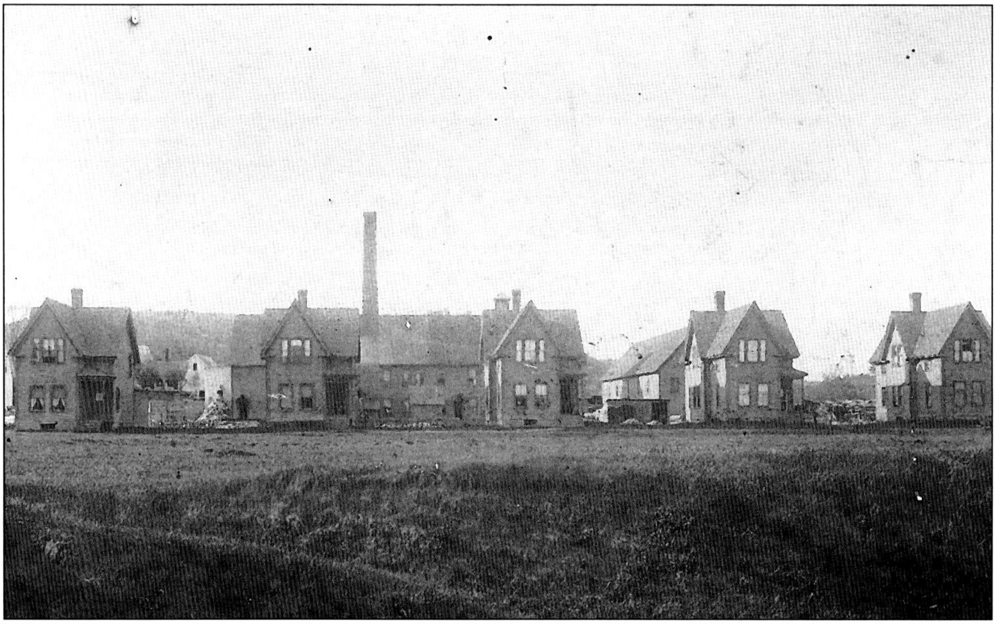

The Foster brothers also built several homes at their mill site which were available to managerial personnel and their families. Those which remain today are now privately owned.

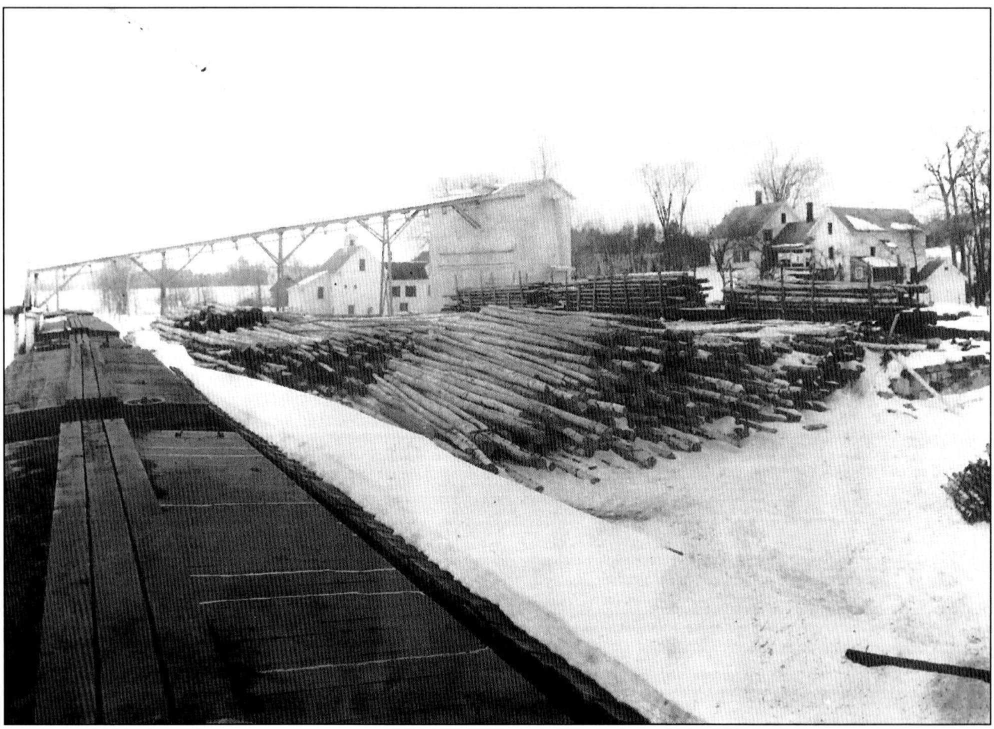

Twenty-five hundred cords of birch logs were brought in to the mill each year by train, much of it from the expansive logging operations in the mountains to the north.

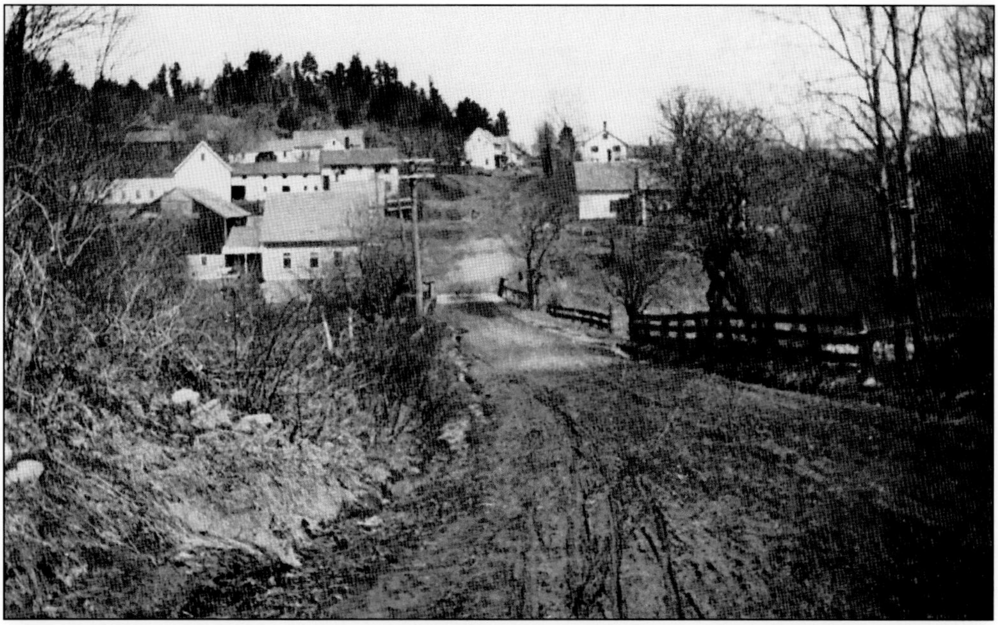

Glove Hollow, shown here looking north on Route 3, was the focus of various small industries in the Lower Intervale section of Plymouth during the early years. These included Captain James Hobart's gristmill and sawmill, a brickyard, and a tan yard, all made possible by water-power from the stream which ran down from Cummings Hill.

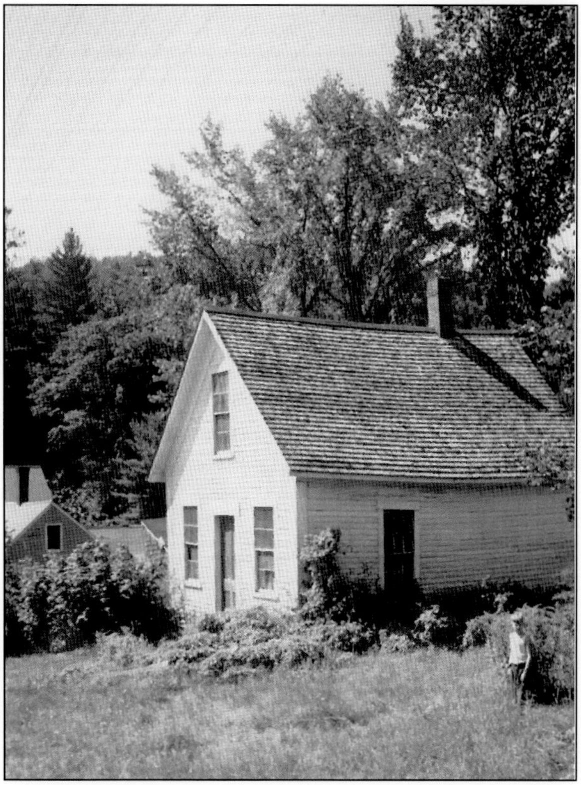

Among the first glove manufacturers in Glove Hollow were Daniel and Henry Currier. They operated their business in the mid-1800s from this small building on the northwest slope. Another of the first glove manufacturers in the Hollow was Jason C. Draper, whose nephew, Jason F. Draper, would join with John F. Maynard to form the internationally known Draper-Maynard Sporting Goods Company.

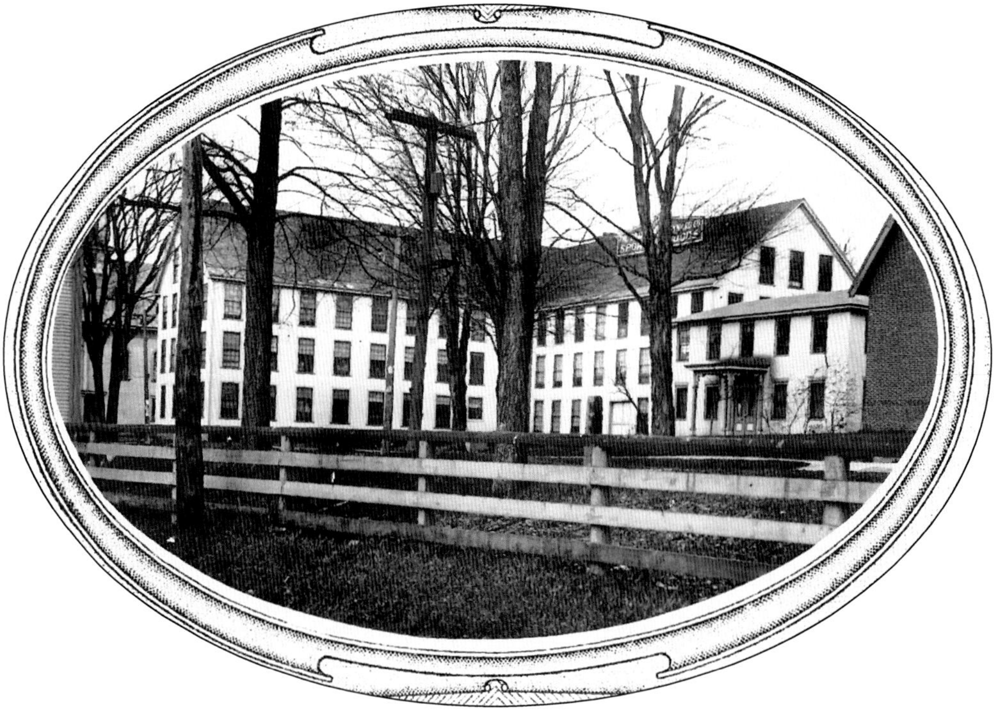

In 1900, Mr. Draper and Mr. Maynard expanded and built a three-story wooden factory on North Main Street in Plymouth. They began to manufacture baseballs and the first padded baseball gloves, soon adding other sporting goods items and employing a staff of 125 men and women.

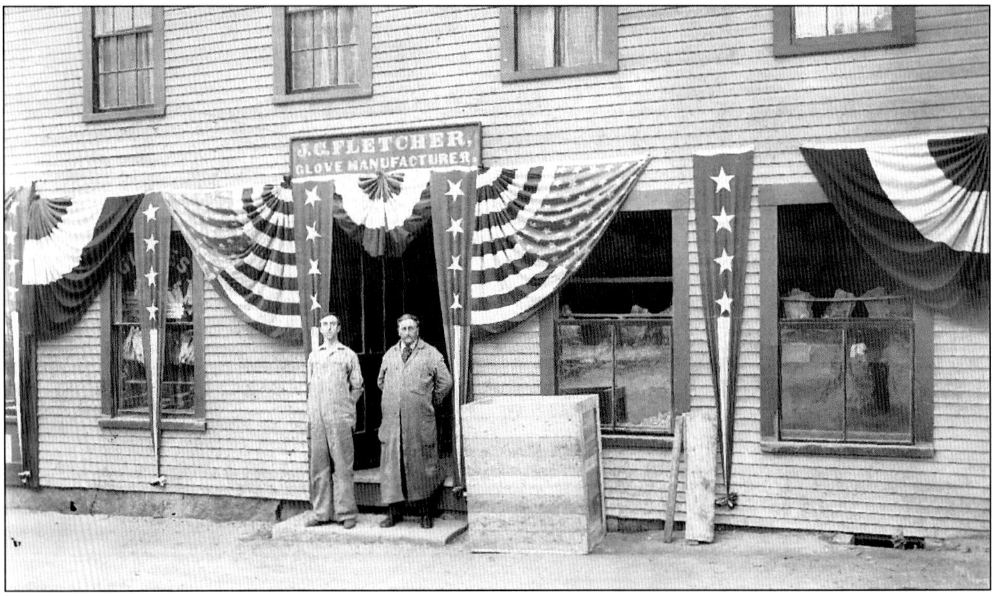

John Gilman Fletcher (right) and his son Fred are shown in front of their glove business at the Tuft's Block. After fire destroyed the property in 1930, the business moved into the Rollins Block above Volpe's Store. The Fletcher's business provided gloves and leather harness material for Admiral Richard Byrd's antarctic expedition.

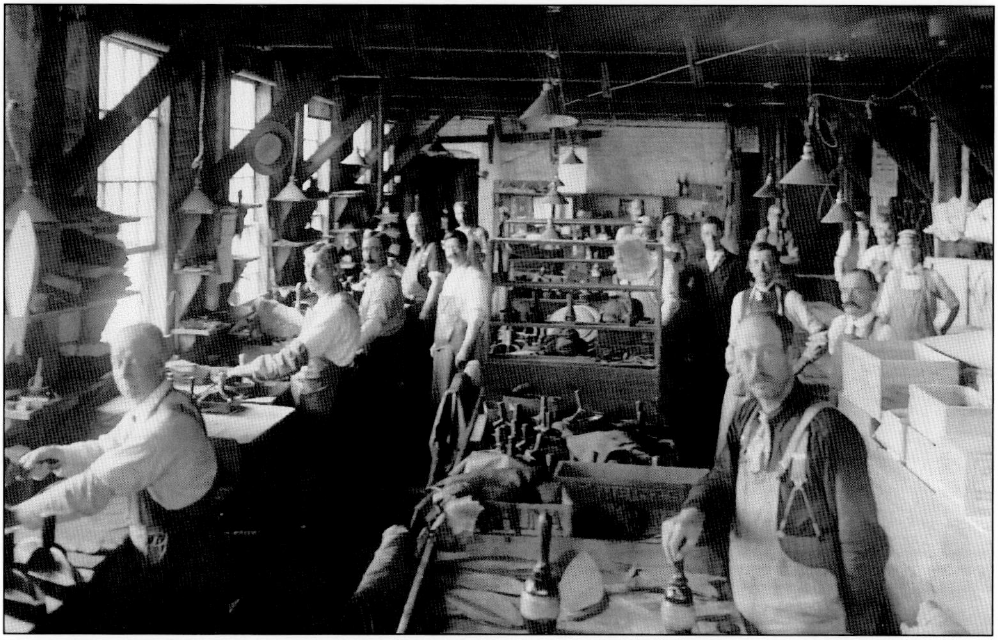

The cutting room in the original D&M factory was a busy area except when all eyes were on the photographer.

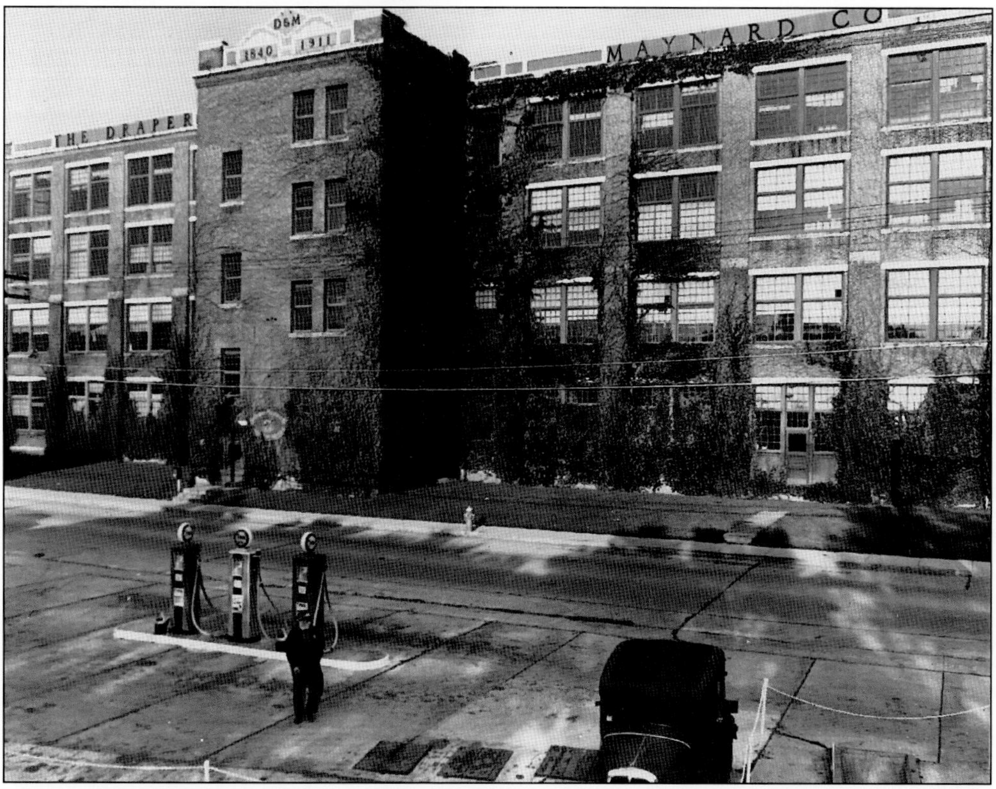

Immediately following a fire in 1910, a new four-story brick building was erected and the Draper-Maynard Sporting Goods Company once again expanded its operations.

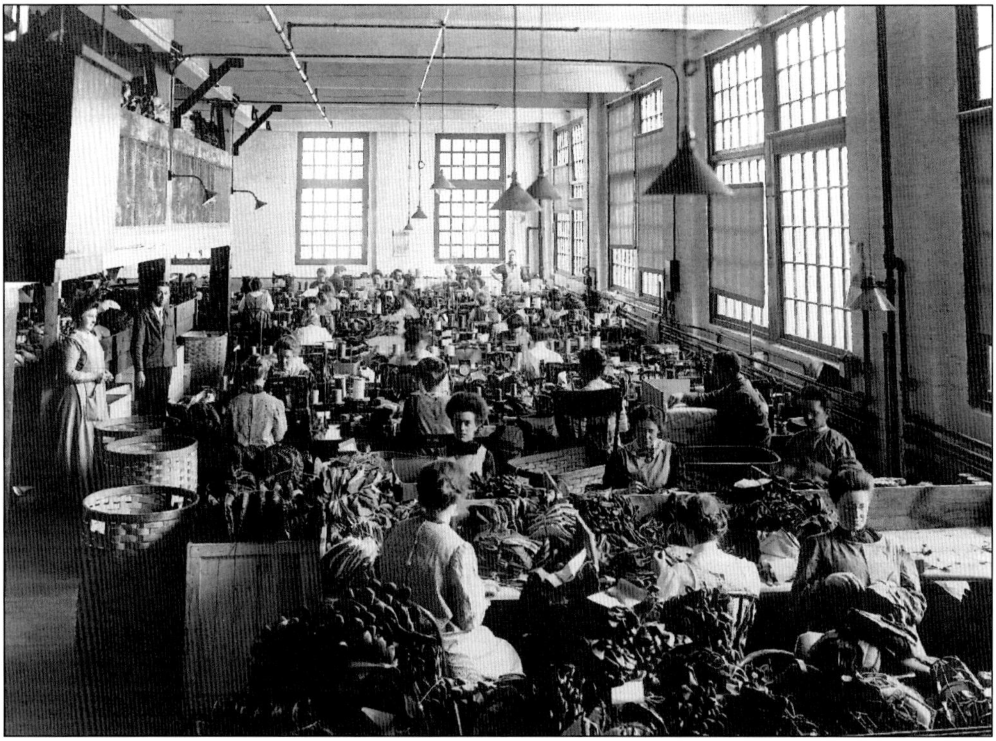

In the new building, the sewing room (above) and the packing room (below) were kept busy, as were the many local women who sewed baseballs at home, laboriously using iron clamps, large needles, and heavy thread—hard work, indeed.

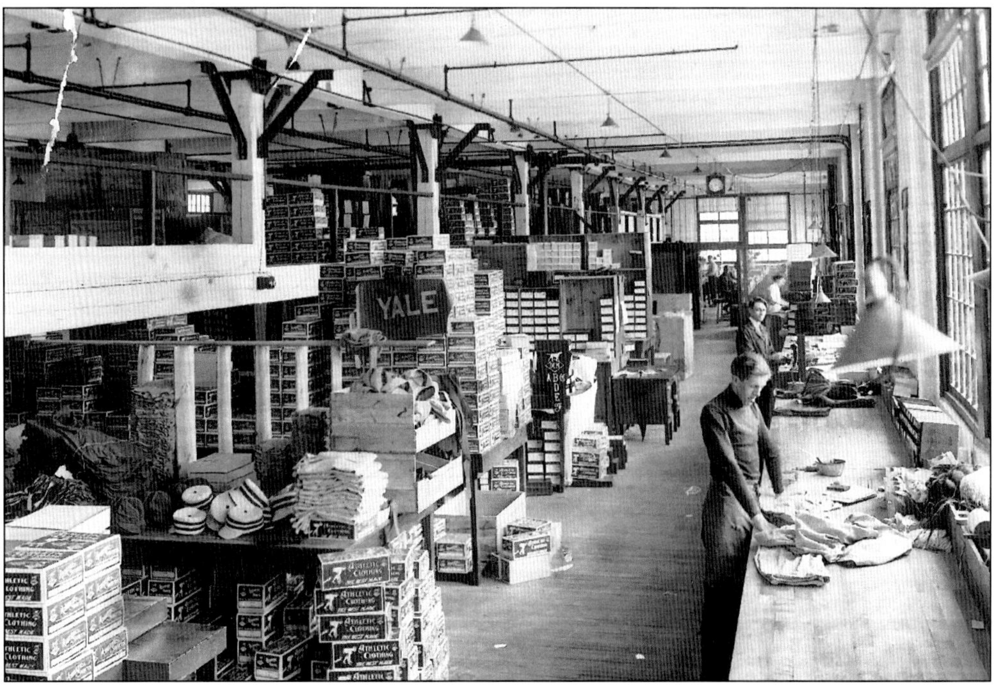

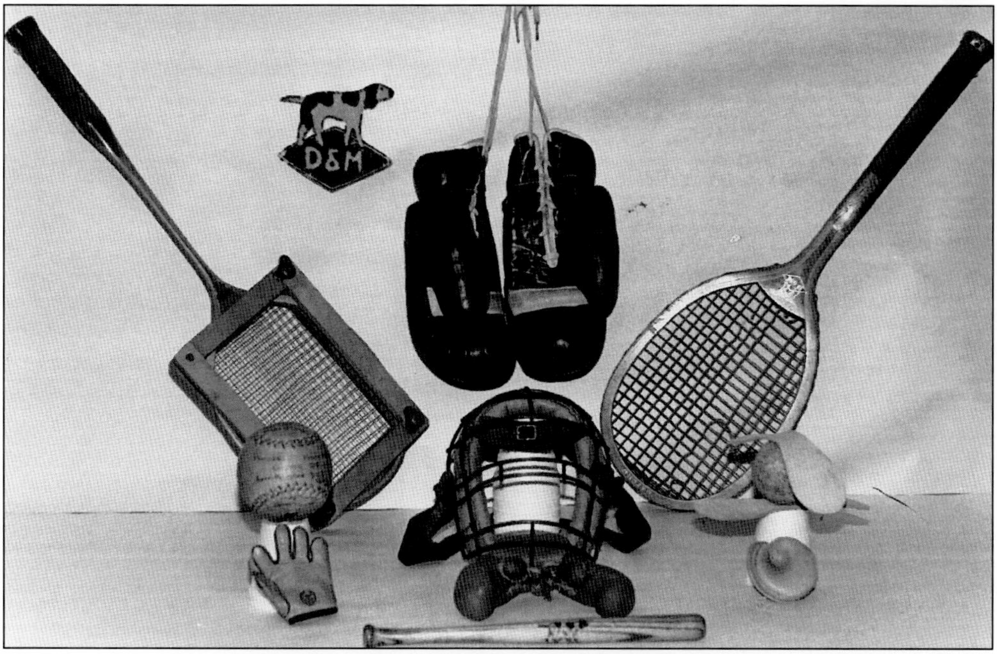

These are just a few of the items made by Draper-Maynard under the sign of "The Lucky Dog." The well-known trademark came about when John Maynard's bird dog, Nick, wandered into a meeting and someone said, "There comes our trademark." Nick's picture was copyrighted, and in 1916 the trademark was expanded with the copyrighting of a remark by Babe Ruth of the Boston Red Sox. He referred to a teammate's glove as " one of the Lucky Dog kind."

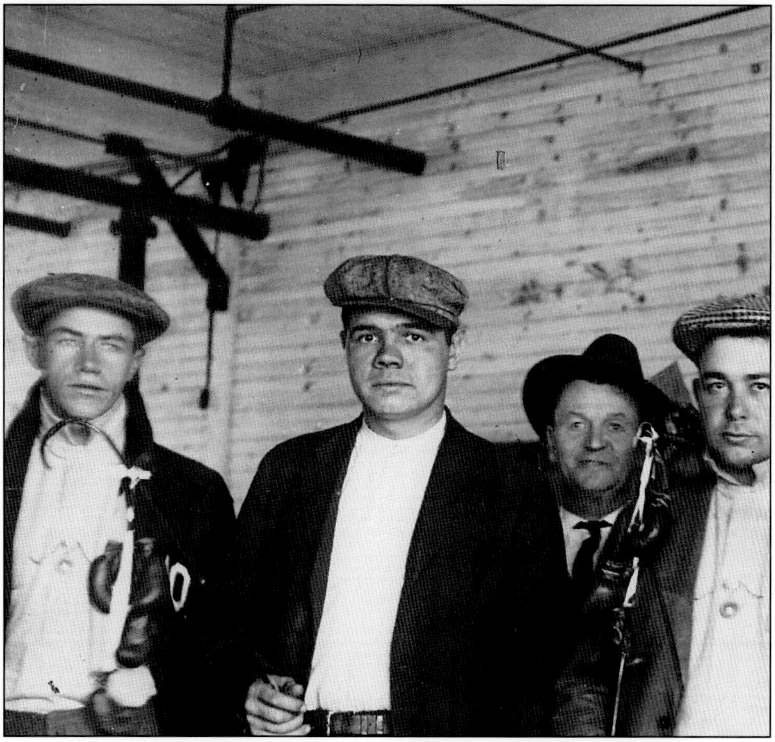

Members of the Red Sox team, along with the Babe, often came to Plymouth to personally pick out their gloves and make suggestions for improvements.

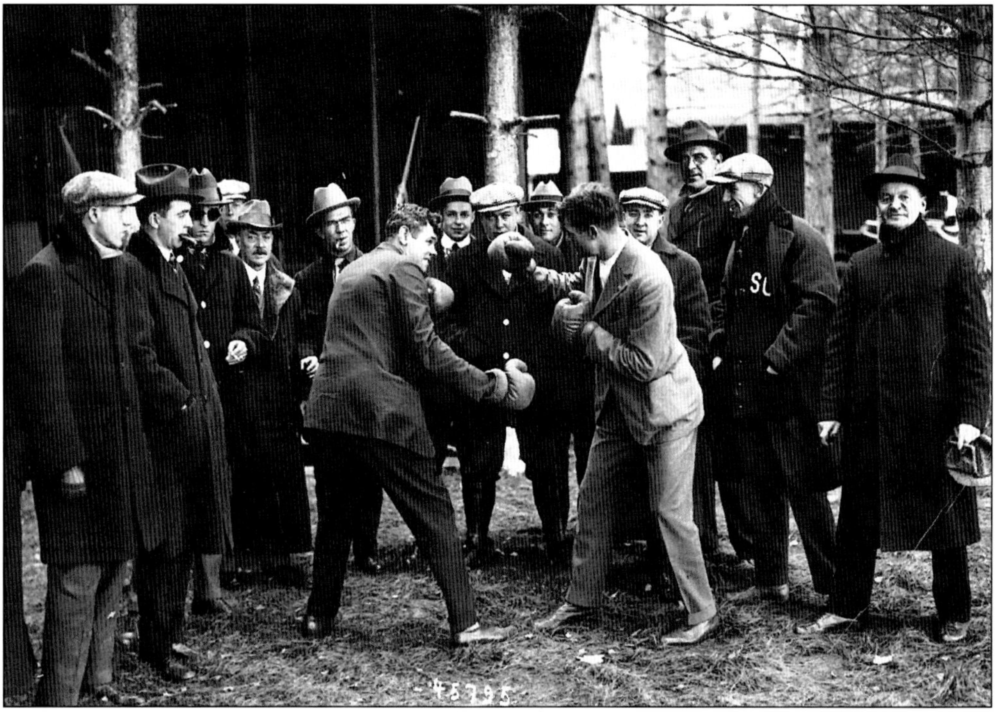

Red Sox team members were often entertained at the Maynard camp on Squam Lake, where Babe Ruth induldged in some sparring, using boxing gloves of the "Lucky Dog Kind."

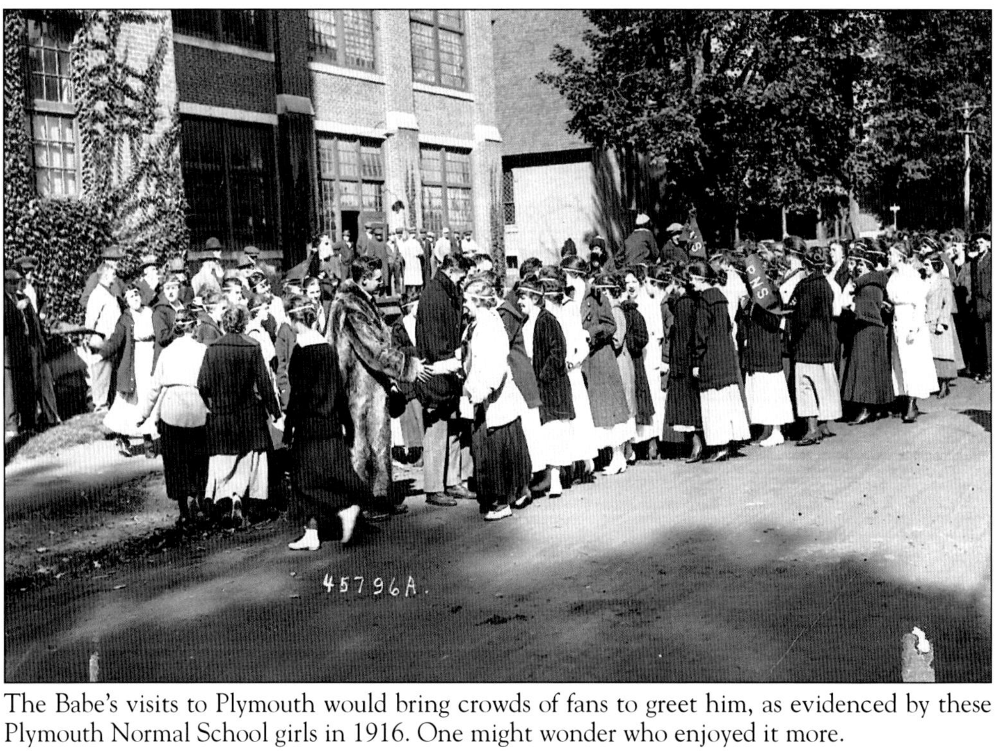

The Babe's visits to Plymouth would bring crowds of fans to greet him, as evidenced by these Plymouth Normal School girls in 1916. One might wonder who enjoyed it more.

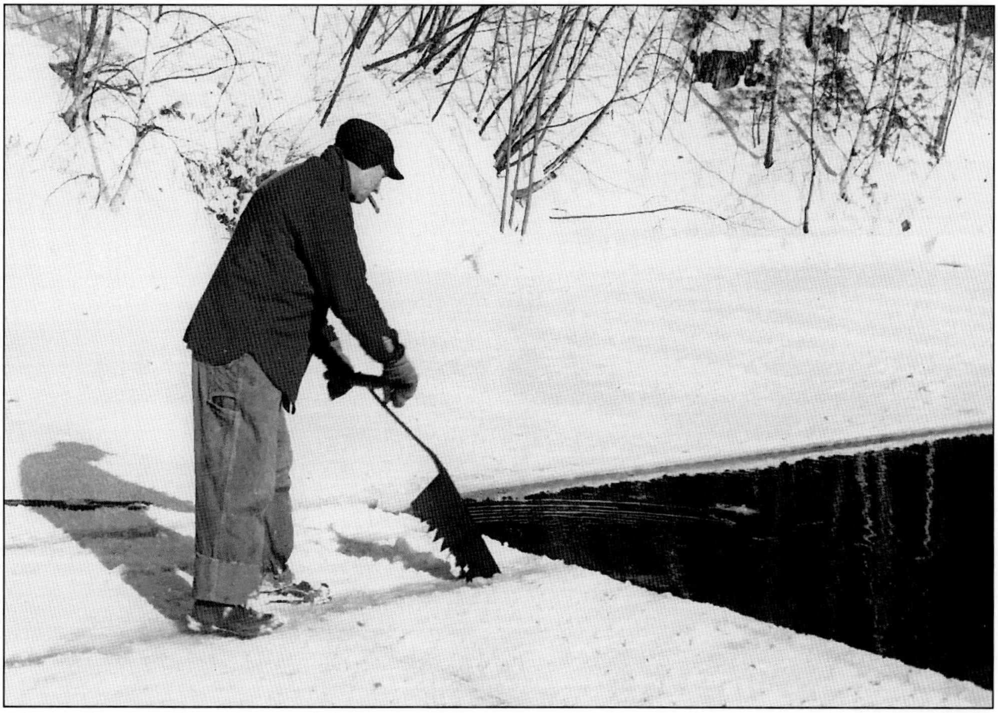

The ice business began around the turn of the century at Fox Pond, created when Plummer Fox dammed the Hazeltine Brook, which ran through his pastureland. These pictures from February 1954, when the business was owned by Philip Knowles, are indicative of the processes used throughout its existence. Using a 5-foot hand saw, Cephas Ransom cuts ice blocks, which will be floated to the storage house.

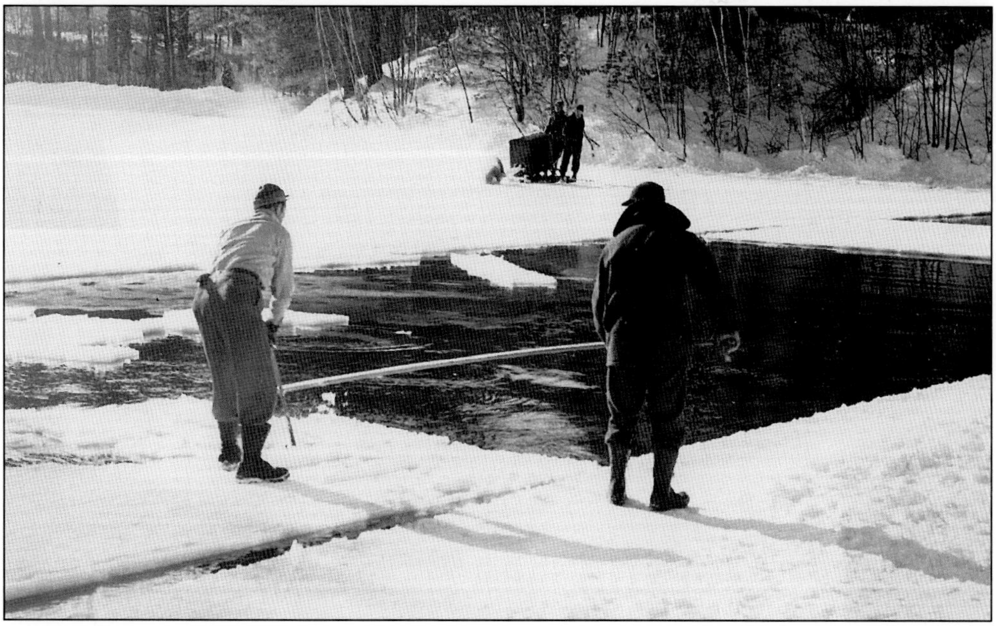

Owner Philip Knowles and Ivan Russell maneuver ice blocks onto the ramp at the storage house.

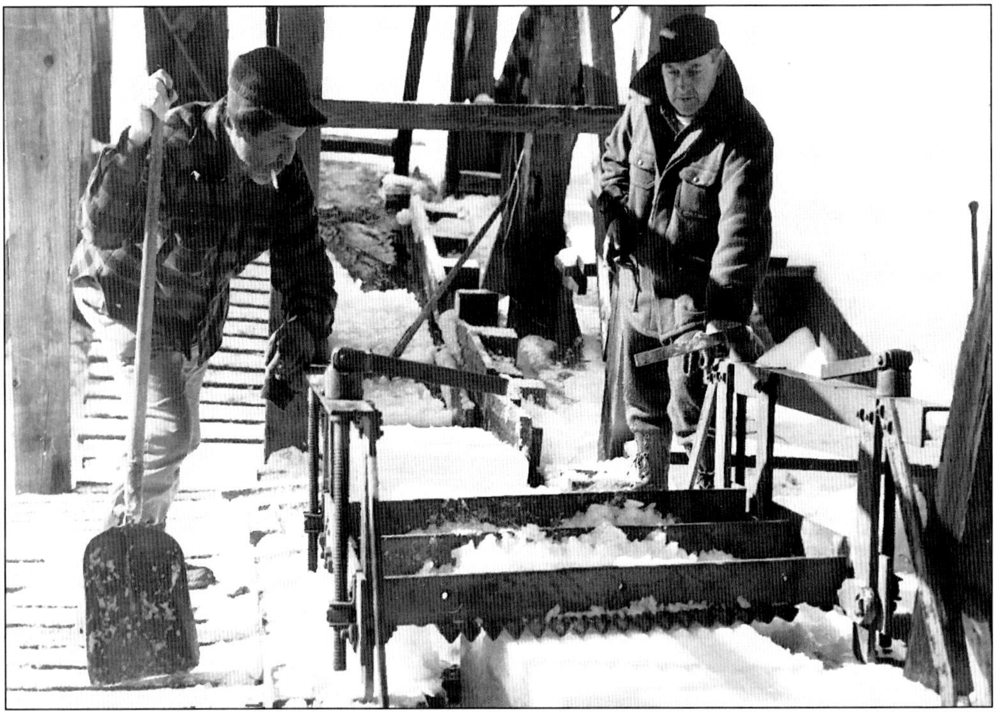

Mr. Knowles and John Pike are shown guiding the ice blocks through the shaver, shaping them for easy stacking.

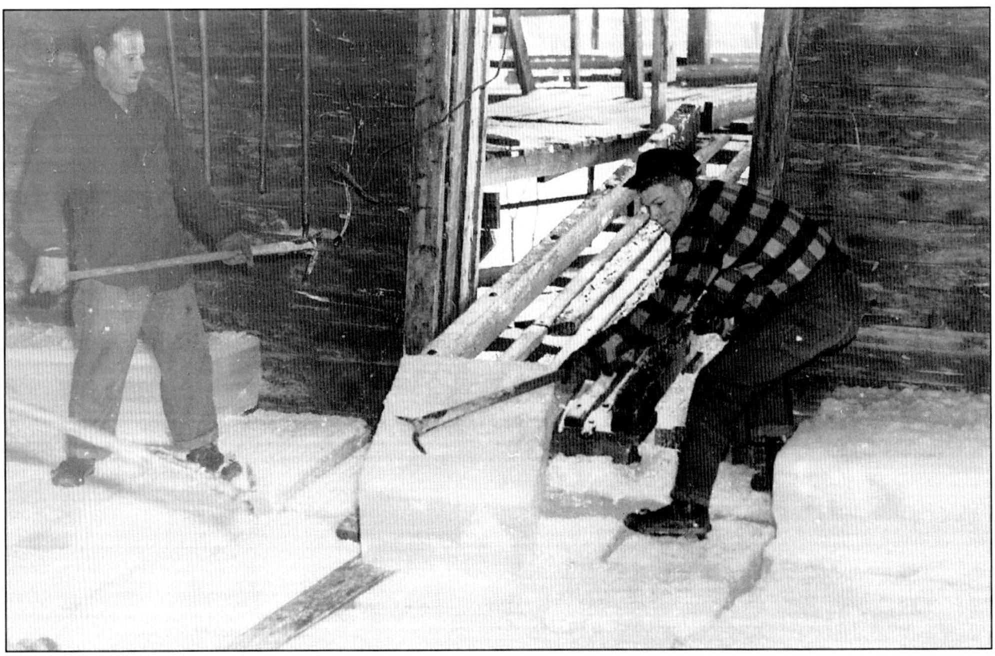

Joel Knowles "wings" ice blocks into layers in the storage house. The top layer was covered by 1 to 2 feet of hay for insulation. This kept the ice through the summer, ready to supply homes, businesses, and hotels in the area. With modern cooling systems and the deterioration of the plant, the icehouse closed in the late 1950s.

Four

SPECIAL EVENTS

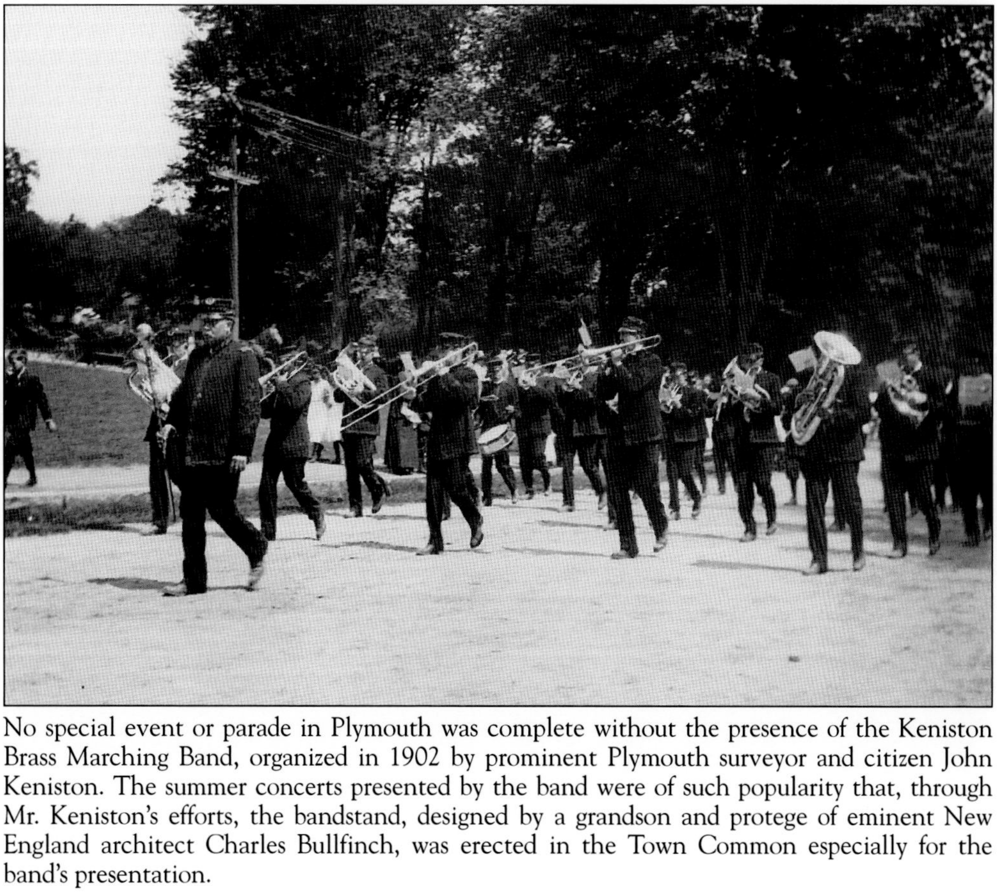

No special event or parade in Plymouth was complete without the presence of the Keniston Brass Marching Band, organized in 1902 by prominent Plymouth surveyor and citizen John Keniston. The summer concerts presented by the band were of such popularity that, through Mr. Keniston's efforts, the bandstand, designed by a grandson and protege of eminent New England architect Charles Bullfinch, was erected in the Town Common especially for the band's presentation.

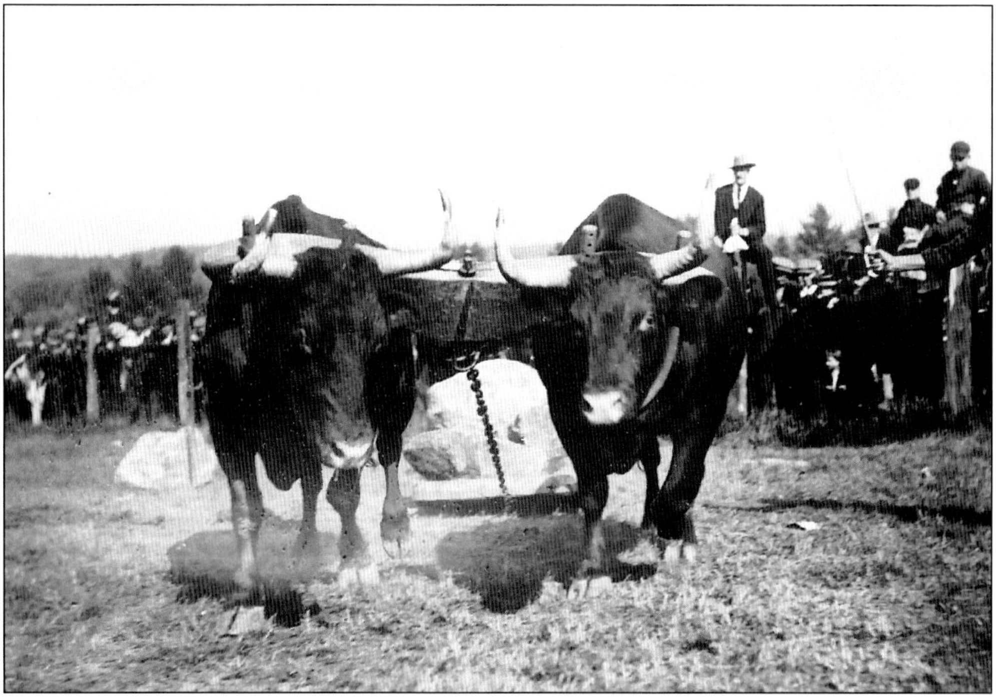

In 1871, Alfred Cook leased land presently consisting of the Fairgrounds to the Grafton County Agricultural Society. Nearly every year since, an agricultural fair has been held on the premises. Folks came to show off their animals or to compete in the various livestock, farm product, and cooking competitions. The oxen shown here are pulling a large stone on a stone boat while being observed by an attentive audience. Such contests have remained favorites at the Plymouth Fair throughout the years.

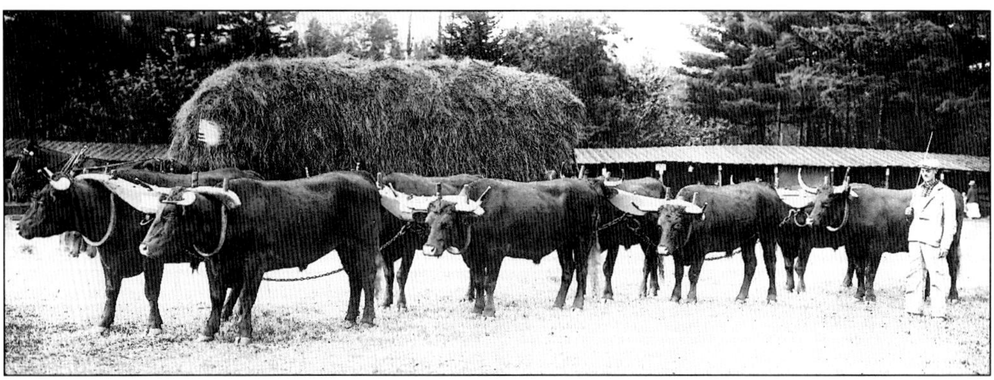

William Wheet of Rumney was one of many farmers in the area who took pride in exhibiting his animals at the Plymouth Fair. Well known for his expertise in training oxen, he is shown here with a team of eight oxen decked out in the American flag for the annual parade. The old cattle sheds and a hayrick are in the background.

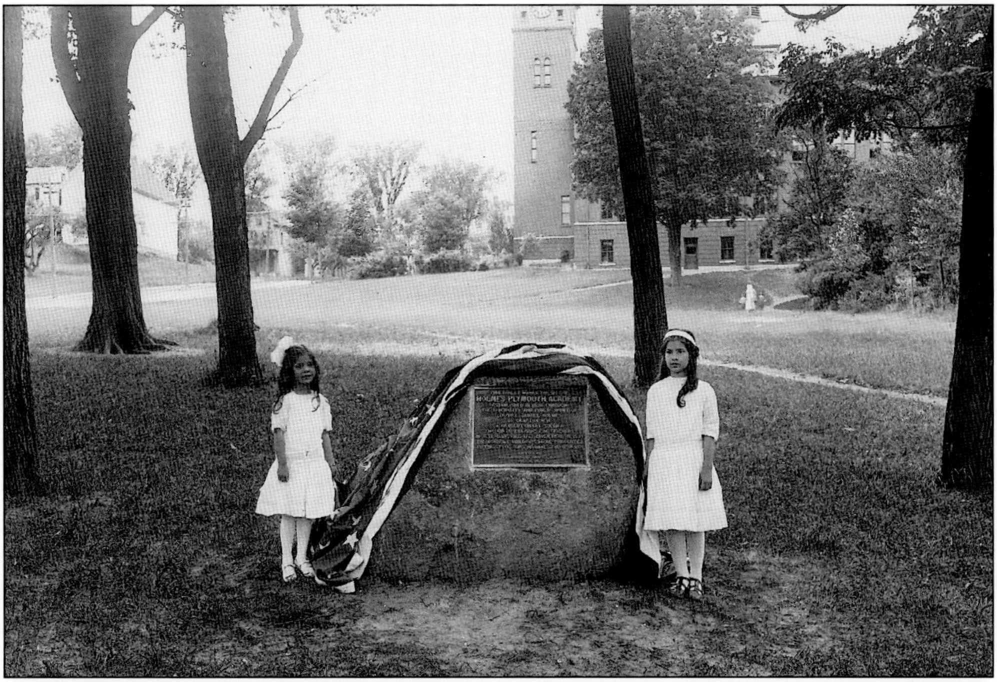

During the celebration of Plymouth's 150th anniversary, a bronze plaque memorializing the site of the Holmes Academy (predecessor of the Plymouth State College) at the corner of Main and Court Streets was unveiled by Elizabeth Denman and Thorndike Rupert. The boulder is now sited on Court Street across from the Plymouth Historical Society Museum.

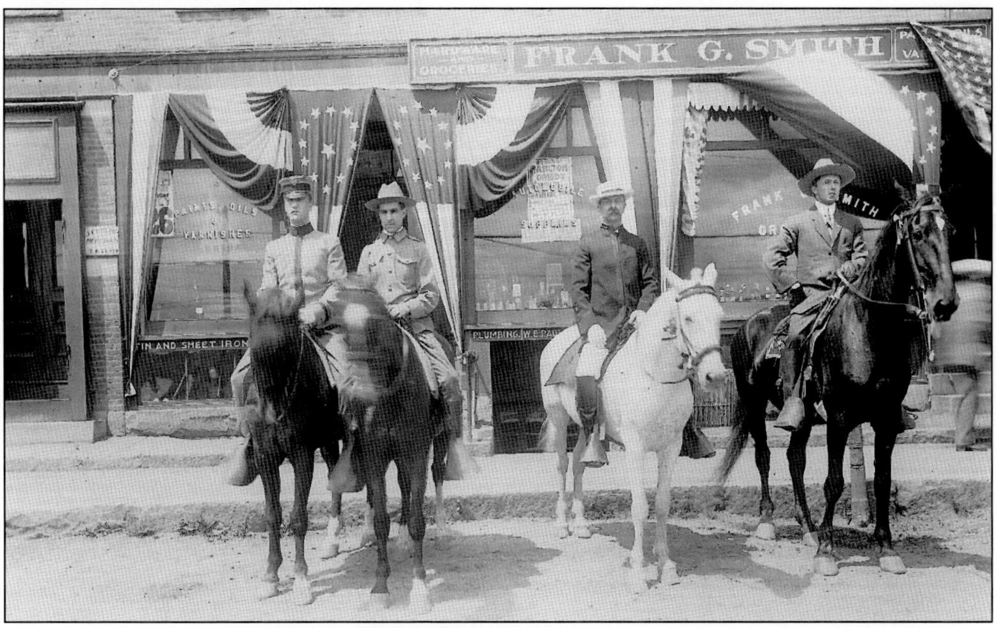

The Grand Parade during Plymouth's 150-year celebration was an extravaganza the likes of which the town had never seen! These three mounted parade marshalls are shown at the corner of Main and Highland Streets. With motor vehicles becoming more commonplace in 1913, the parade was a blend of both horse-drawn and "horseless" vehicles.

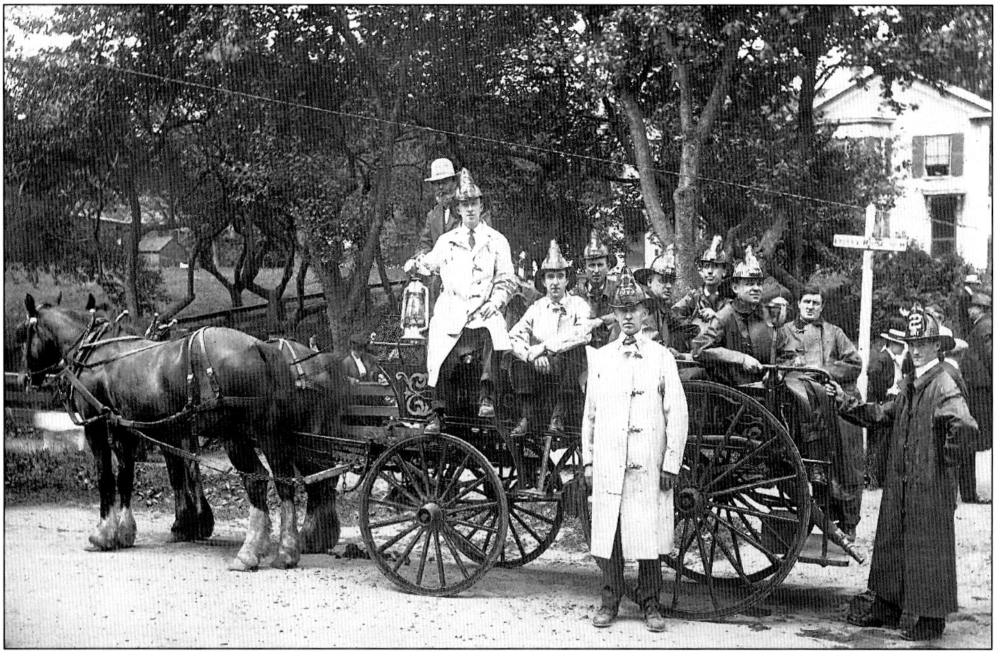

These firemen very likely used extra spit and polish when they readied themselves and their equipment for the 150th anniversary festivities.

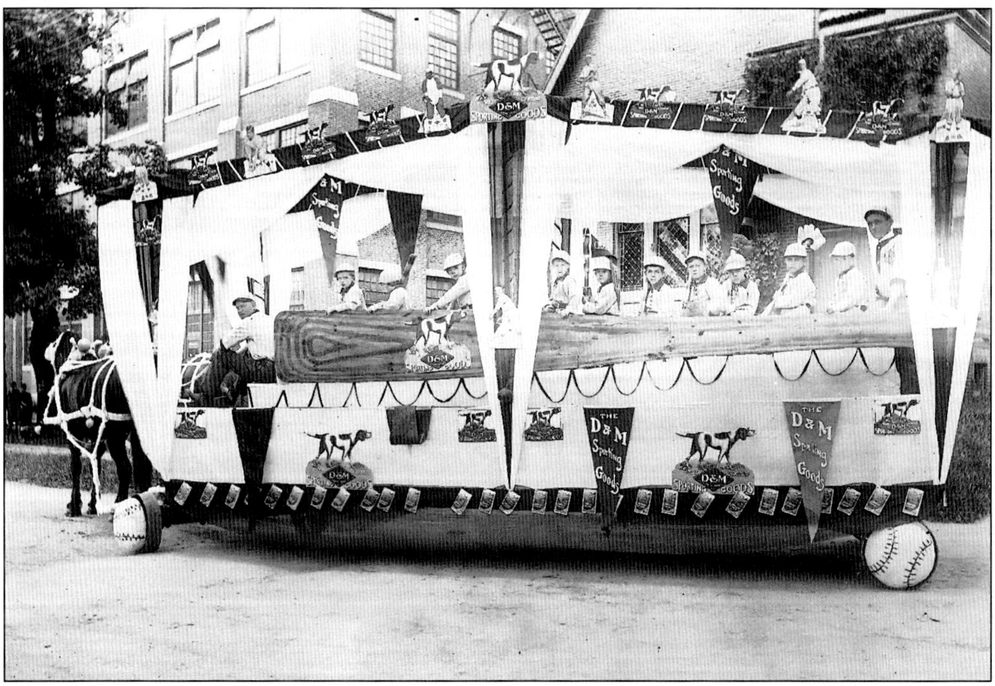

Imagine the excitement for the youngsters riding the Draper & Maynard float in the 150th Anniversary Parade! The "Lucky Dog" logo was prominently displayed, and the cleverly designed baseball wheels carried out the theme of the company's most popular product. The building in the background, only three years old in 1913, was where world-famous sporting goods were manufactured and where many Plymouth residents were employed.

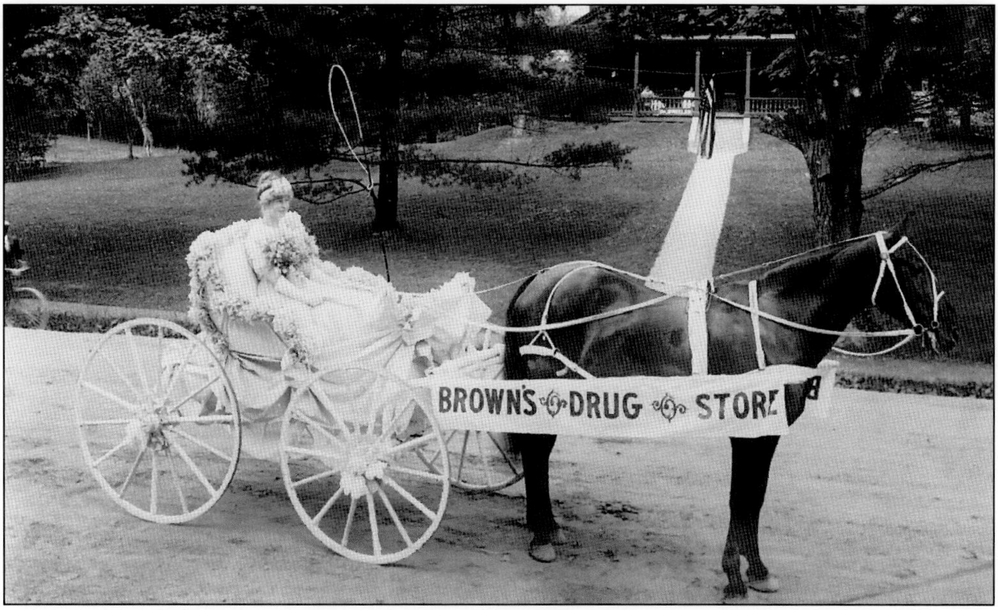

Fred Brown's Drugstore was represented in the parade by a beautifully decorated pink and white carriage with white tack on the horse, driven by Hazel Fern Caldon. Brown's Drugstore was responsible for the printing and distribution of picture postcards and souvenir dishes with scenes of area interest. They are valued parts of collections today.

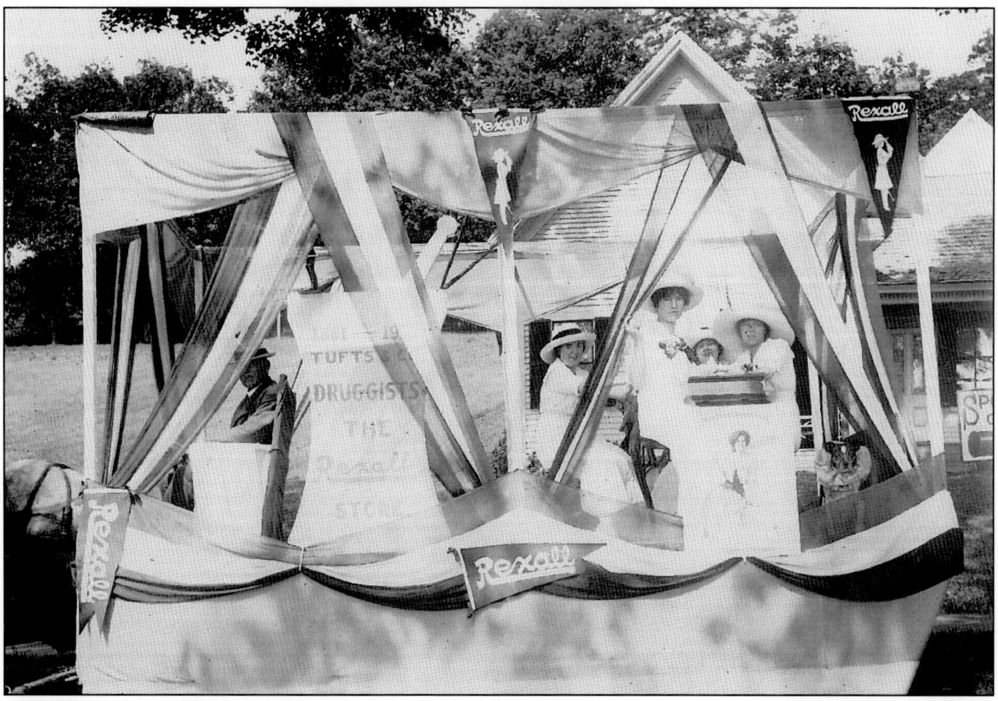

Exhibiting a healthy competition in the drugstore business, these lovely young ladies and their ruffled dog ride proudly on the Tufts' Rexall Drug Store float. For many years, the Tufts family manufactured many medicines in Plymouth, and their various bottles and vials are seen in several fine collections.

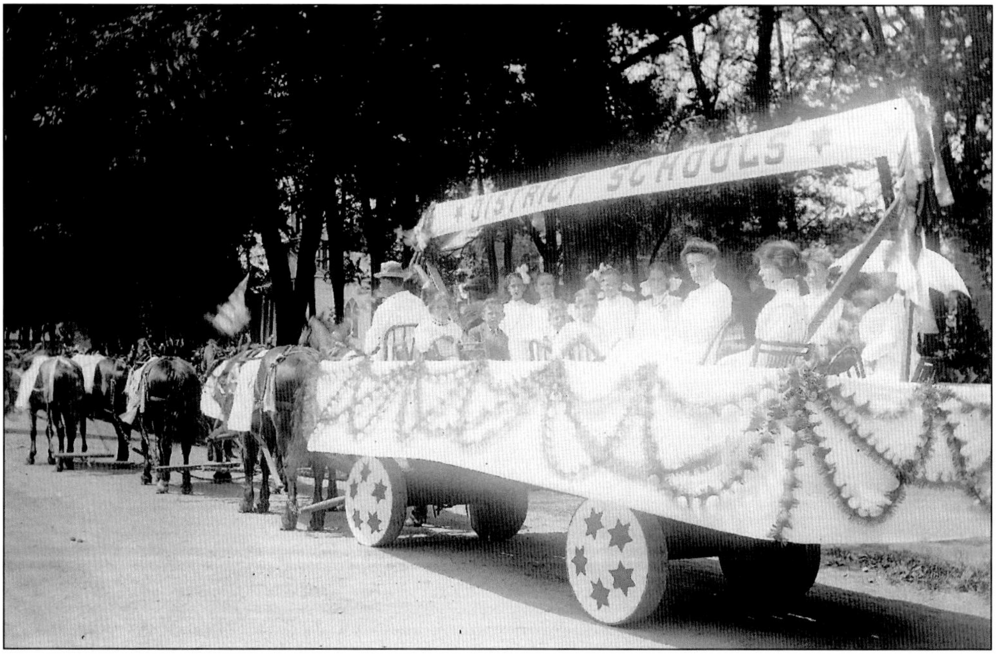

Drawn by three teams of horses, the very long float representing the District Schools of Plymouth was one of the most outstanding in the parade. The joint effort of the more than ten schools operating in the town in 1913 exemplifies the importance the citizens of Plymouth put on its schools and the pride taken in them.

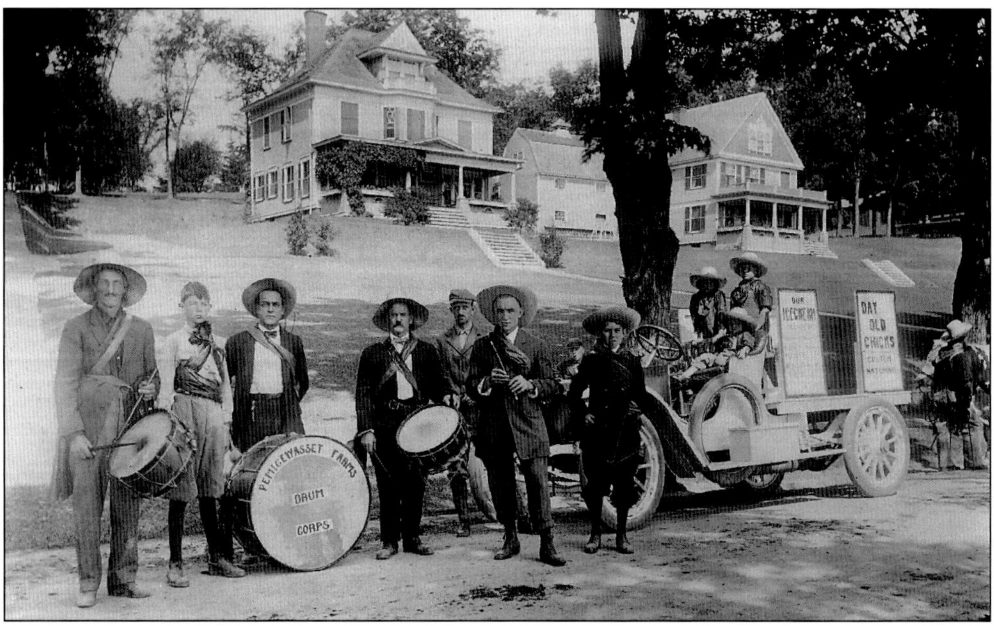

The Pemigewasset Farms Drum Corps is lined up at the corner of Main and Merrill Streets with a sign-bedecked farm truck carrying local youngsters. It is followed by a bovine representative of the farming community.

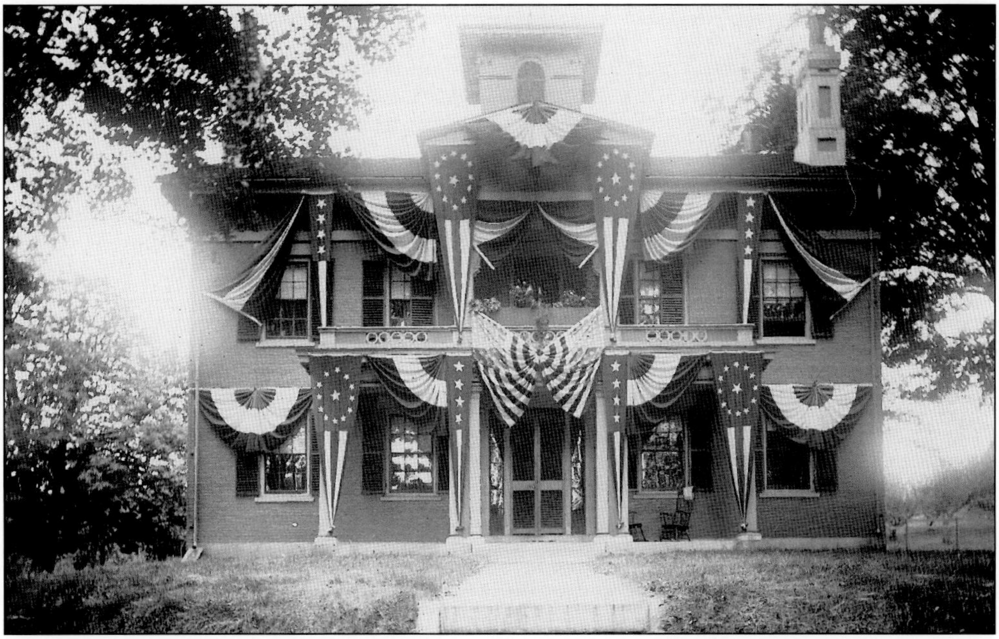

The 150th anniversary celebration in Plymouth was many months in preparation. Providing bunting, flags, and other decorations for the town must have taken a great deal of time and energy. Even private homes joined in the spirit of the event as evidenced by the elaborately decorated Russell house on Highland Street with its grand view of the Common.

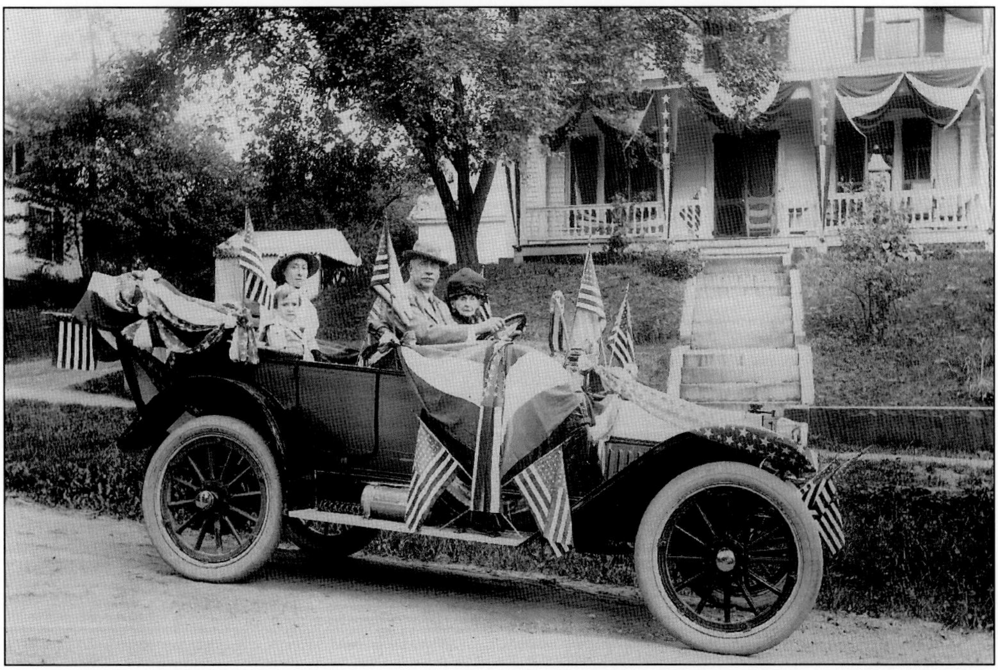

A very young Charles Bowles sits in a proudly decorated automobile with his parents, Dr. and Mrs. George Bowles, and his grandmother, Mrs. Mary Anne Bowles. They are in front of the handsomely bedecked family home on Russell Street, apparently ready to join in the parade just down the hill on Main Street.

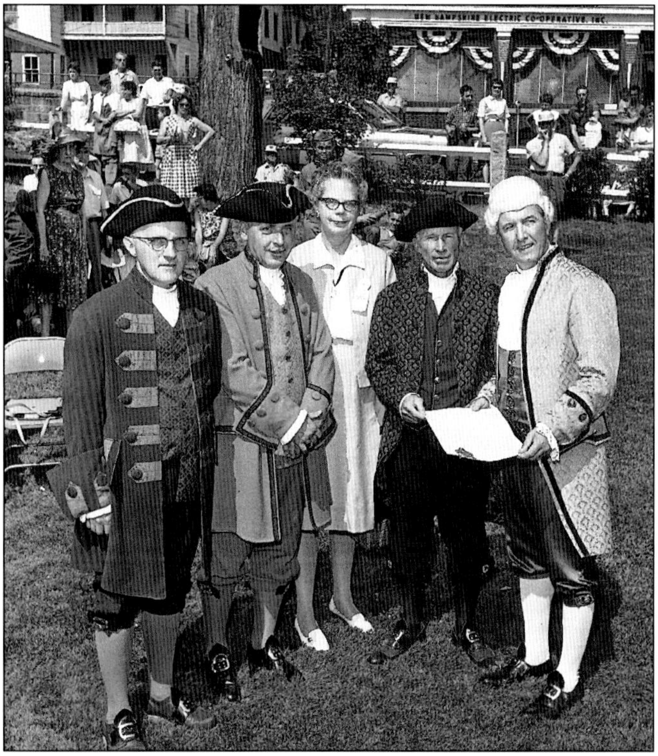

The bicentennial celebration on July 13, 1963, was the product of many months of discussion, planning, and organization by the Bicentennial Commission. Shown here is the chairman of the commission, M. Suzanne Loizeaux, with, from left to right, Selectmen Lee Buckland, Edward Pettingill, and Fred C. Tobey Jr. acting as the original grantees, receiving the Town Charter from Governor John King, who portrayed Royal Governor Benning Wentworth. With this reenactment of the establishment of Plymouth, the ceremonies began.

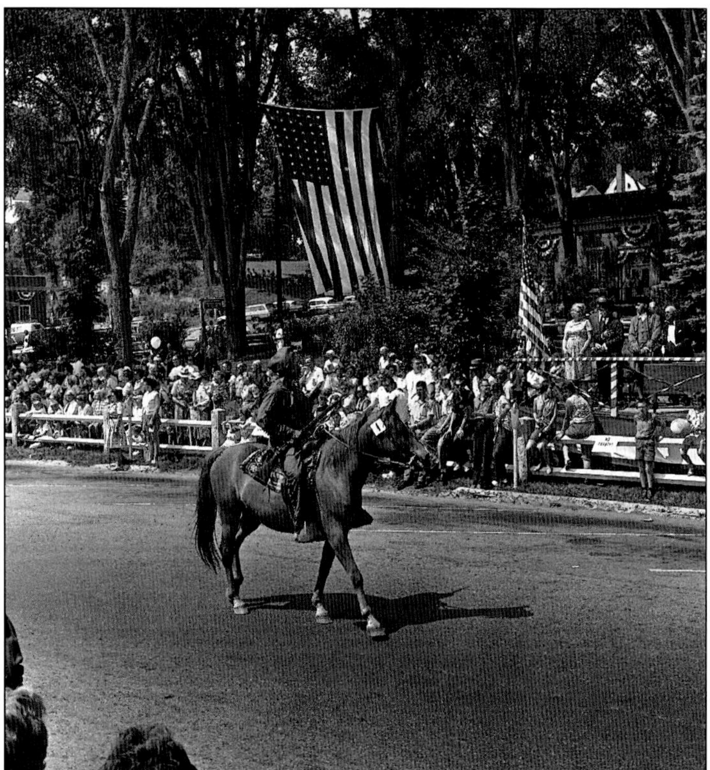

Astride his Morgan horse and representing Captain David Webster, who was a scout and surveyor for the settlers of Plymouth and himself later a settler, Arnold W. Spencer acted as parade marshall. A true Plymouth native, Mr. Spencer traced his family back 5 generations to one original settler on his father's side and four on his mother's side. Following Mr. Spencer came the 70 units and bands which made up the two-hour-long Grand Parade.

July 13, 1963, turned out to be a sunny, pleasant, and extremely hot day. Watson A. Rand, splashing happily in a bathtub on the A.M. Rand Co. float, was perhaps the most comfortable person in the whole parade.

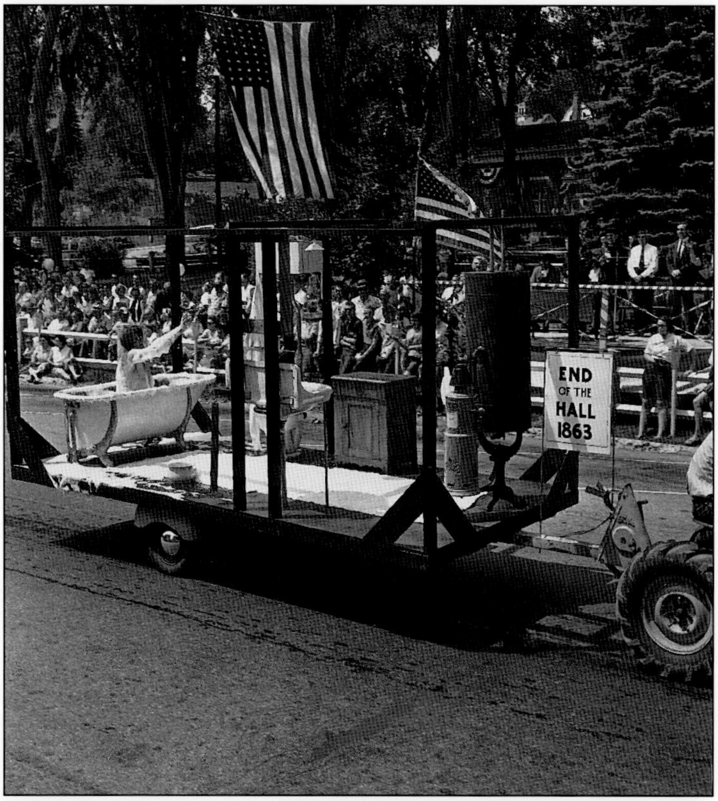

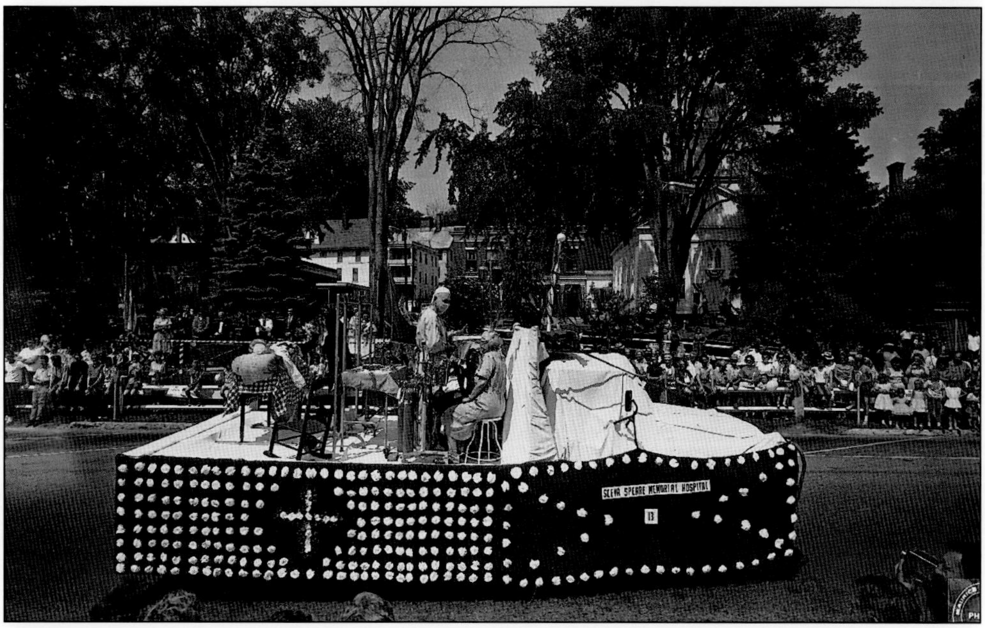

The Sceva Speare Hospital float won a prize and was not only attractive, but also entertaining. Doctors and nurses from the hospital depicted contrasting methods of surgery in 1763 and 1963 (in a somewhat exaggerated form).

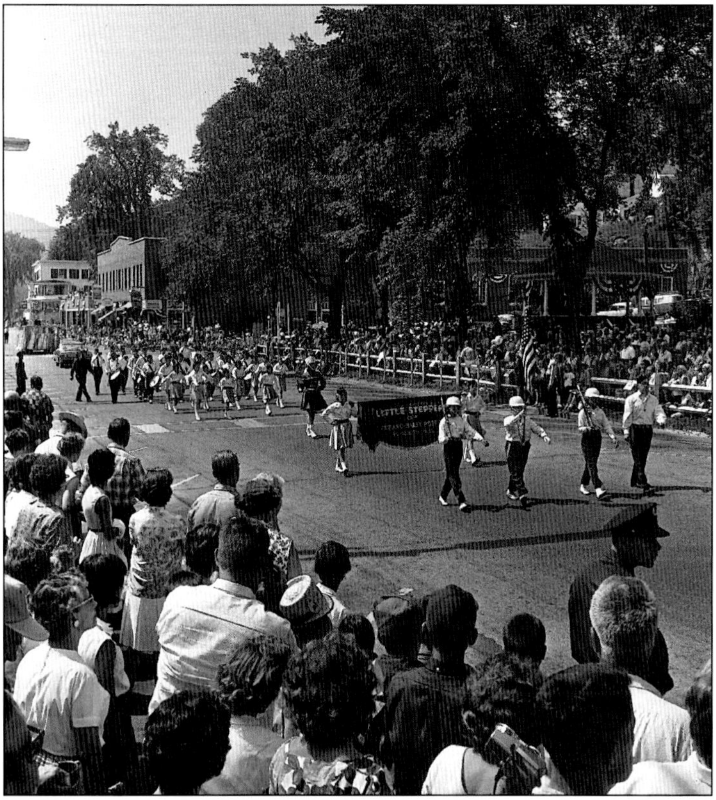

Fifty youngsters, ranging in age from 8 to 14 years and directed by Harold Freeman, called themselves "the Little Steppers Drum and Bugle Corps." They were sponsored by American Legion Post #66 of Plymouth. The group won an honorable mention in the Best Marching Musical Unit category. Mr. Freeman, director for many years of the band concerts given on the Common in the summer, also composed "The Bicentennial March." It was played for the first time in front of the reviewing stand.

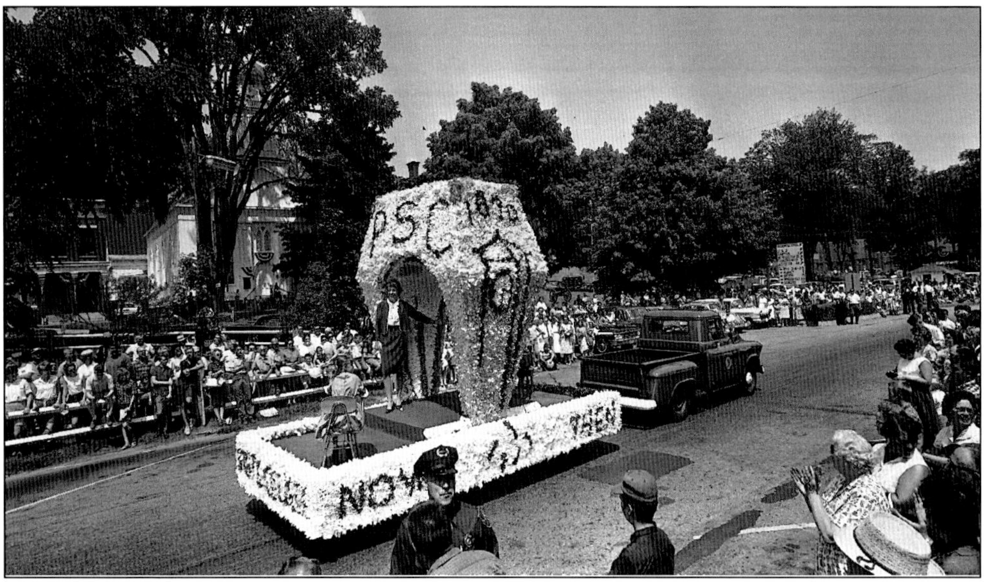

The Plymouth State College float was judged to be the best in the parade and depicted the "Then and Now of Education." It contrasted methods of education of the 1870s, when the Plymouth Normal School came into being, with those of the 1960s.

Circuit riders were often the preachers in the early days of the area. A scene of the preacher ministering to a family in front of their log cabin is depicted by members of the Plymouth Methodist Church.

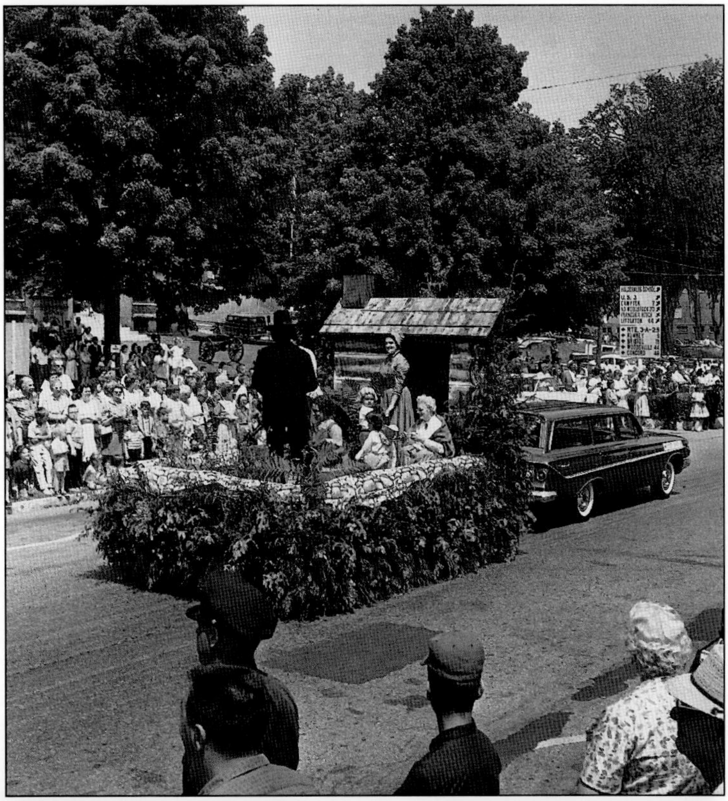

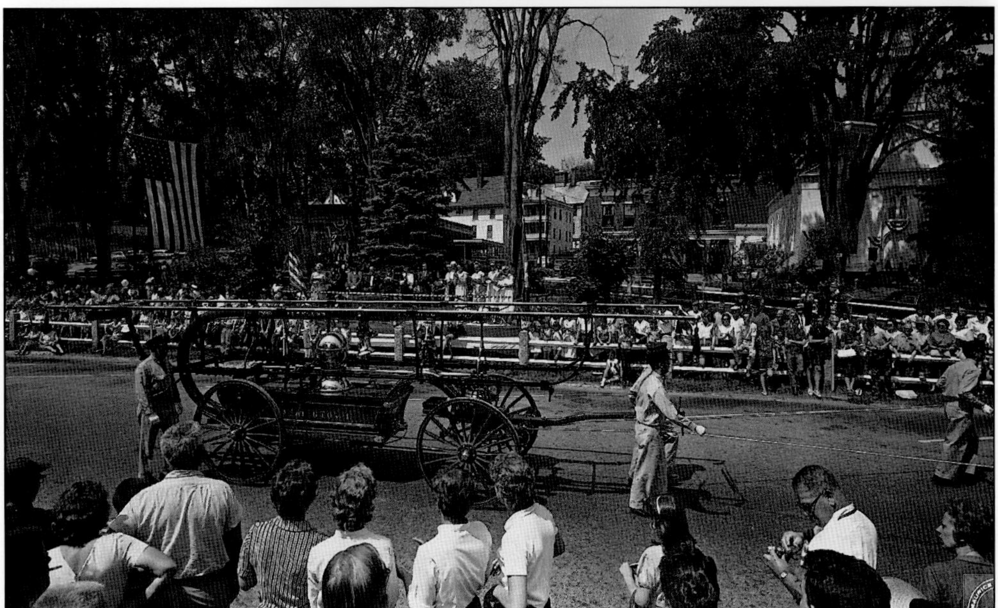

The North Kingston, Rhode Island pumper proudly pulled by its volunteers was judged Best Appearing Unit in the Fireman's Muster Division. This was one of many such units from around New England that marched in the parade and later competed in the New England Fireman's Muster on the playing fields across the Pemigewasset River in Holderness.

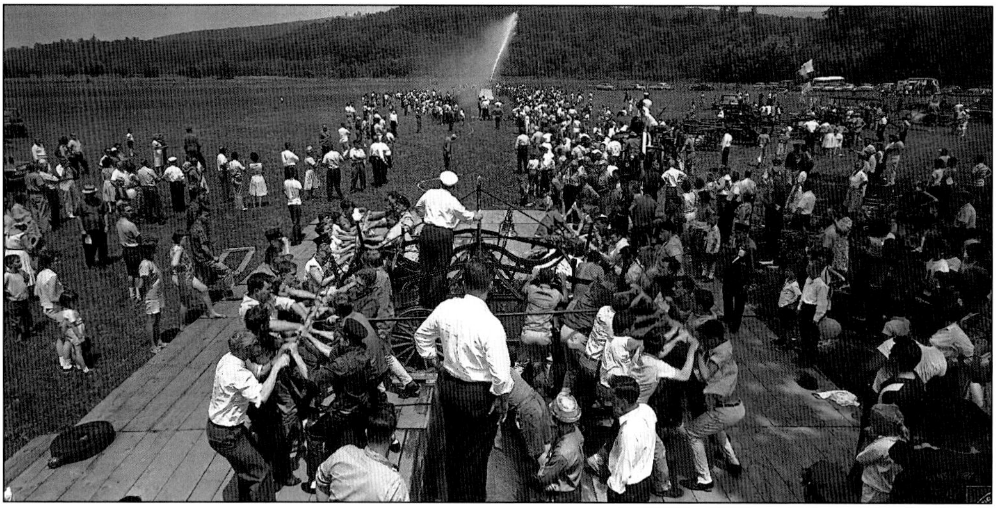

At the Fireman's Muster, the winning unit (and also the oldest, being built in 1856) was manned by its New Boston, New Hampshire crew and several willing bystanders, shooting a stream of water a distance of 195 feet. Even with today's modern fire equipment, which can direct streams of water great distances and with great force, it is still impressive what could be done with hand pumpers and manpower.

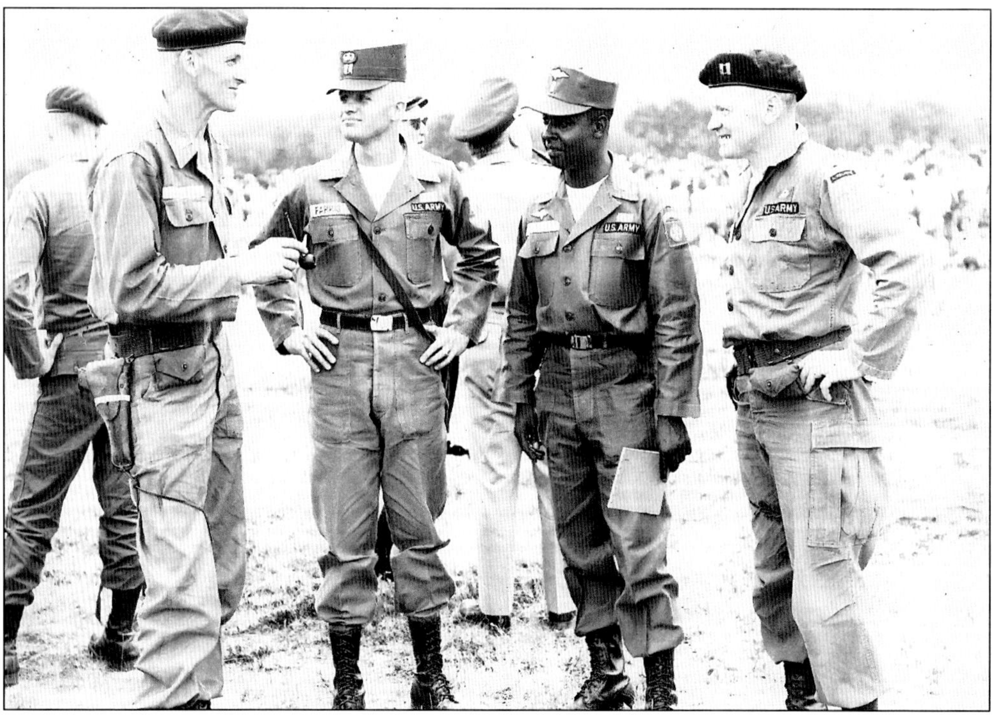

As a part of Plymouth's celebration, a mass parachute demonstration by the U.S. Air Force Reserves from Grenier Field in Manchester was staged over the Plymouth airport on Quincy Road. Fifty men dropped from two "flying box cars" from 1,200 feet before about 3,000 onlookers. While about half landed on the runway, others drifted onto nearby Longview farm and a few ended their fall in treetops. There were no injuries and it was a sight not soon forgotten.

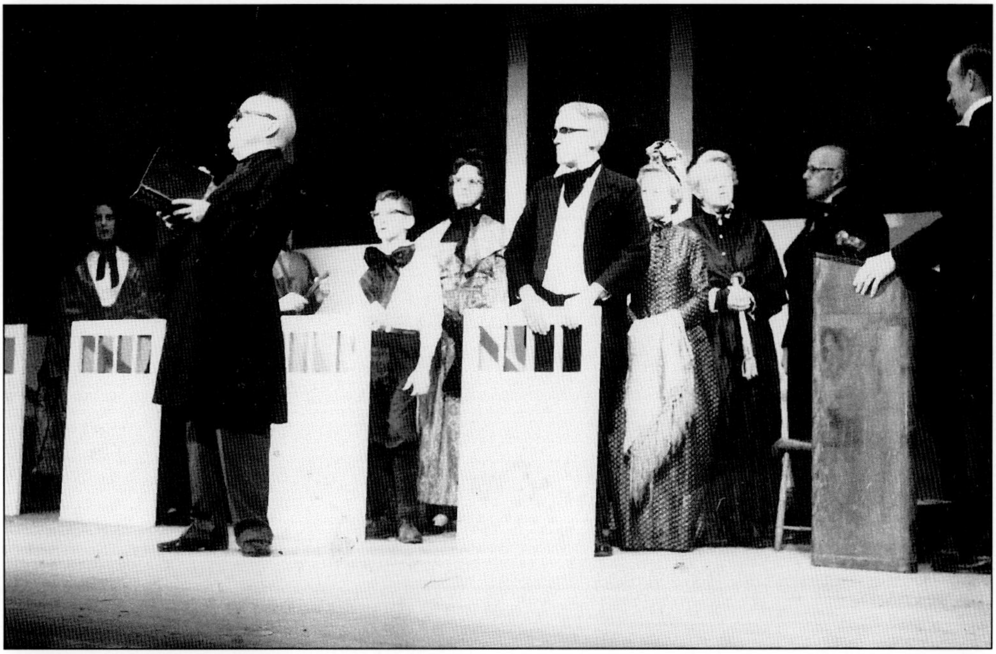

On Sunday, July 14, 1963, citizens of Plymouth, all with entertainment talent, presented a pageant depicting scenes of Plymouth history. Some were serious, some humorous, and all instructional. Written and directed by Lucille Little, it was greatly appreciated by a large audience at the Silver Hall auditorium.

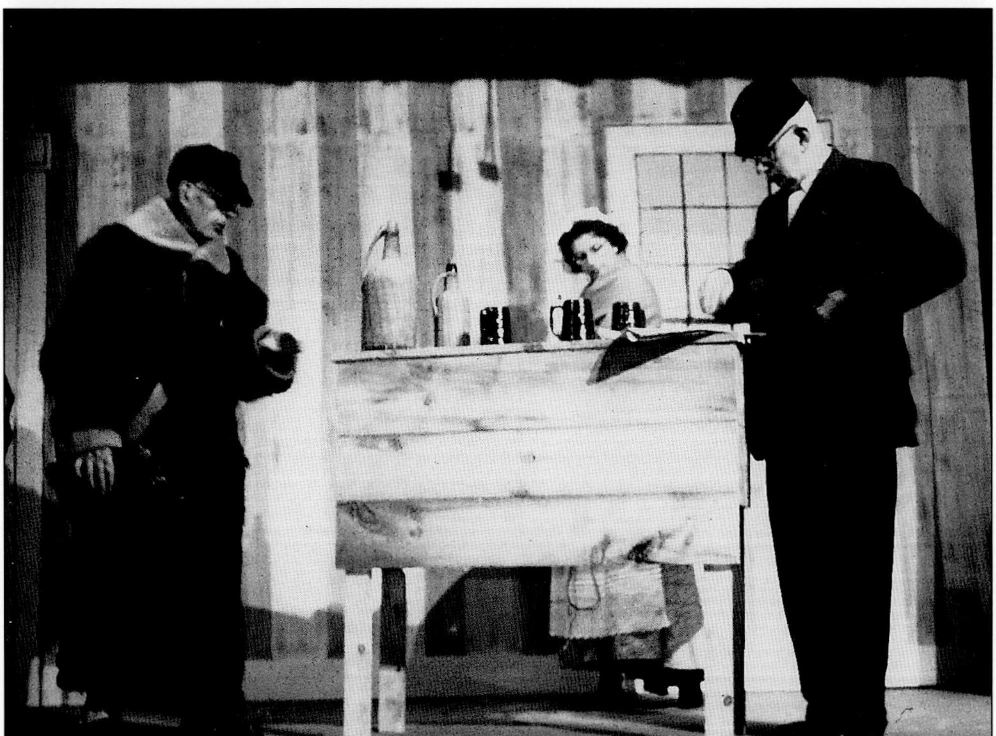

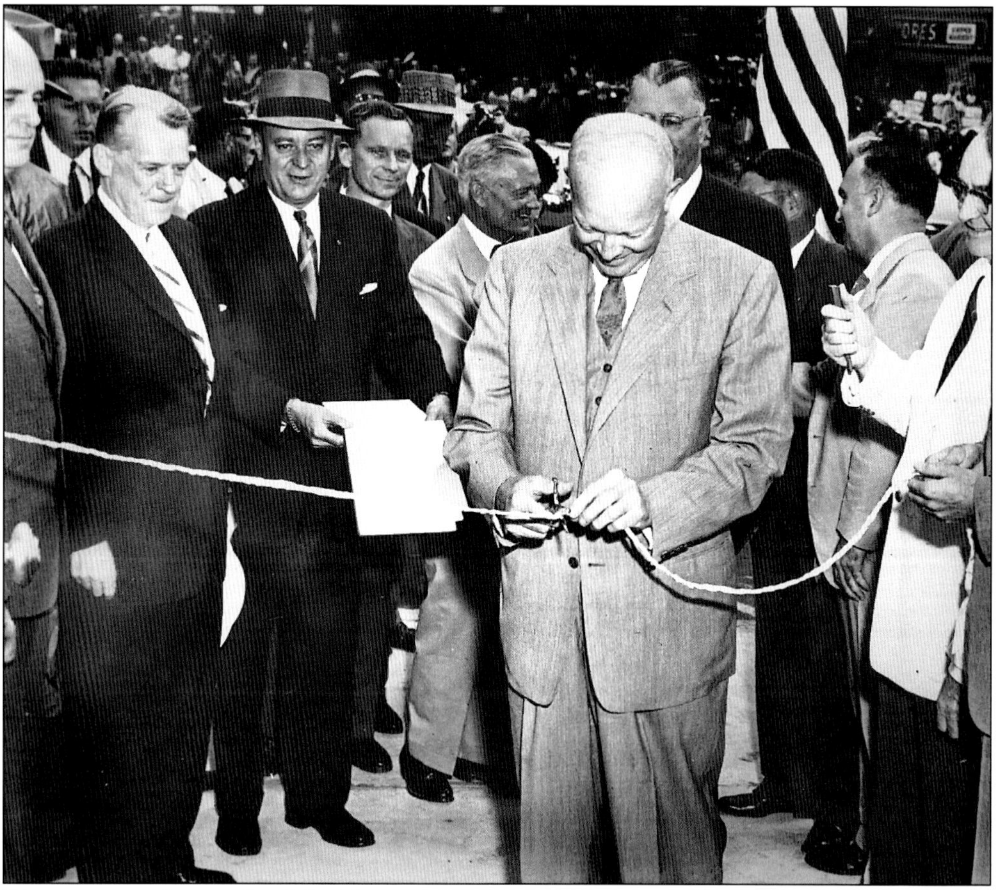

The opening of a new bank building on June 24, 1955, for two longtime Plymouth banking institutions—the Pemigewasset National Bank and the Plymouth Guaranty Savings Bank—was made especially auspicious by the presence of President Dwight D. Eisenhower. President Eisenhower cut the ribbon officially opening the modern building at the foot of Highland Street. Many state politicians and banking officials, including bank president Thomas Gadd, Gov. Lane Dwinell, U.S. Sen. Styles Bridges, Congressman Perkins Bass, Presidential Assistant Sherman Adams, U.S. Sen. Norris Cotton, bank president Bertram Pulsifer, and directors Carl Adams, Bill O'Brien, and John Geyer, shared the spotlight before the President continued northward for a visit to the White Mountains.

Five

SCHOOLS

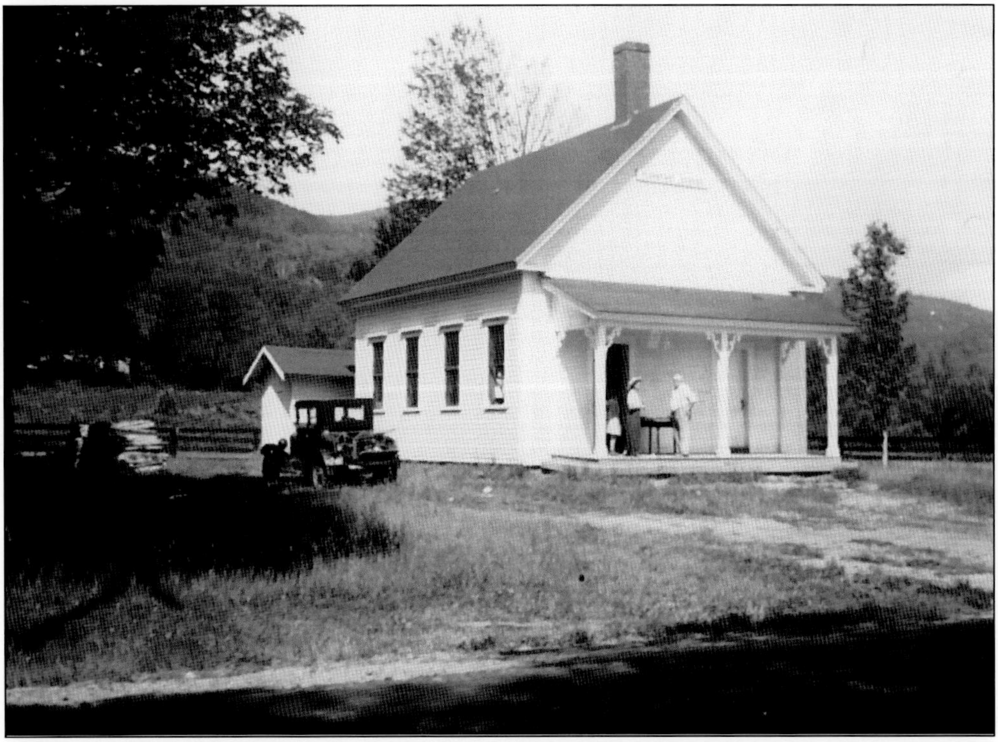

This is a view of Turnpike School on Route 3A South, West Plymouth. Former Harvard president Derek Bok's observation, "If you think education is expensive, try ignorance," may well have been the same thought in the minds of Plymouth's early settlers when they voted in 1774 to divide the town into four districts and "to draw money to be laid out for schooling." Although the number of districts varied over the years, a representative number of the district schoolhouses used well into this century still stand.

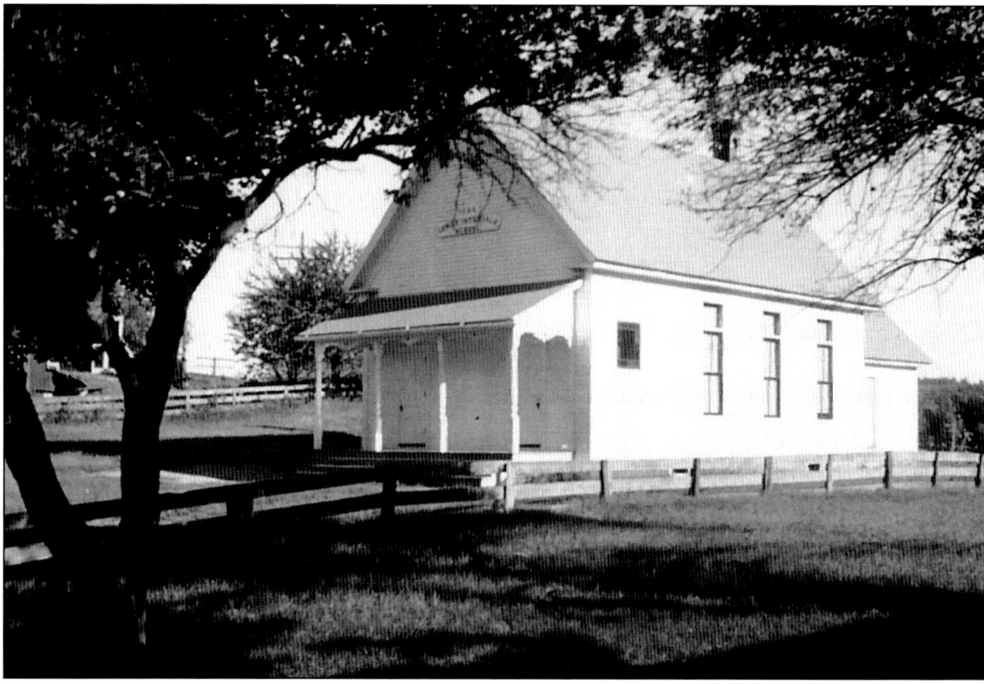

This scene is of Lower Intervale School, near the intersection of Routes 3/25 and River Road.

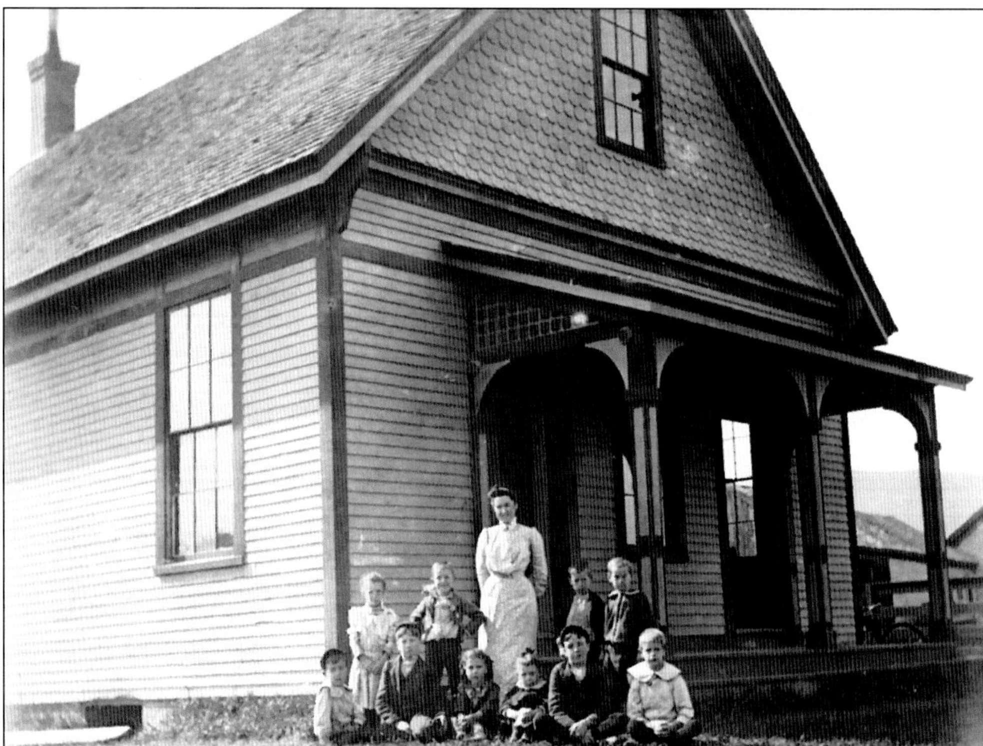

This is the Baker River School near the intersection of old Route 25 and Smith Bridge Road, West Plymouth.

Here, near the intersection of Route 3 on Fairgrounds Road, is the Livermore School.

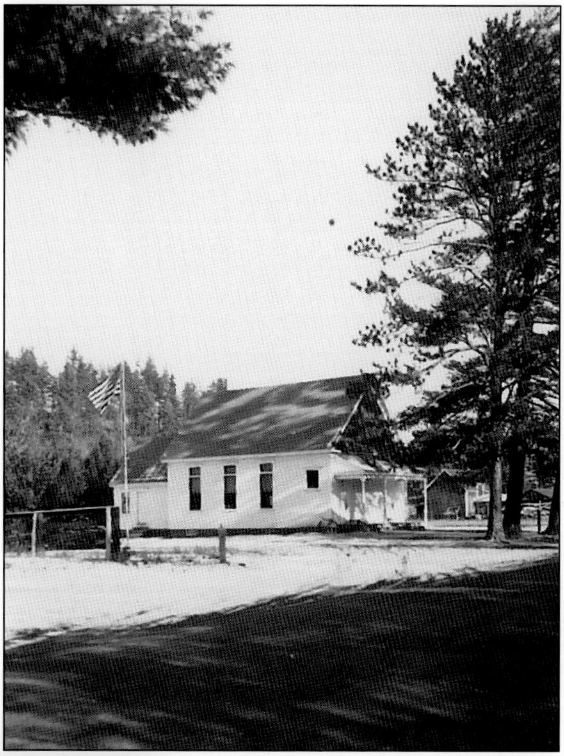

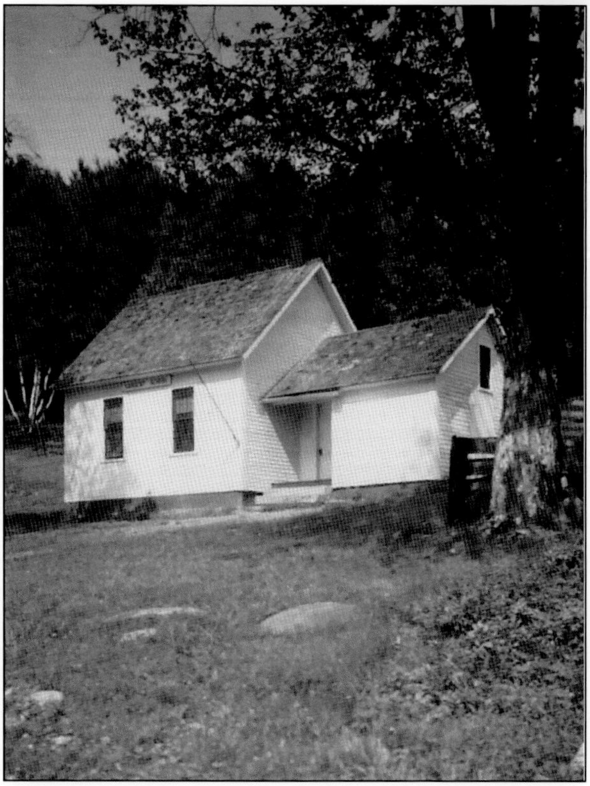

Here is a view of Sargent School on Texas Hill Road between New Hebron Road and Old Hebron Road.

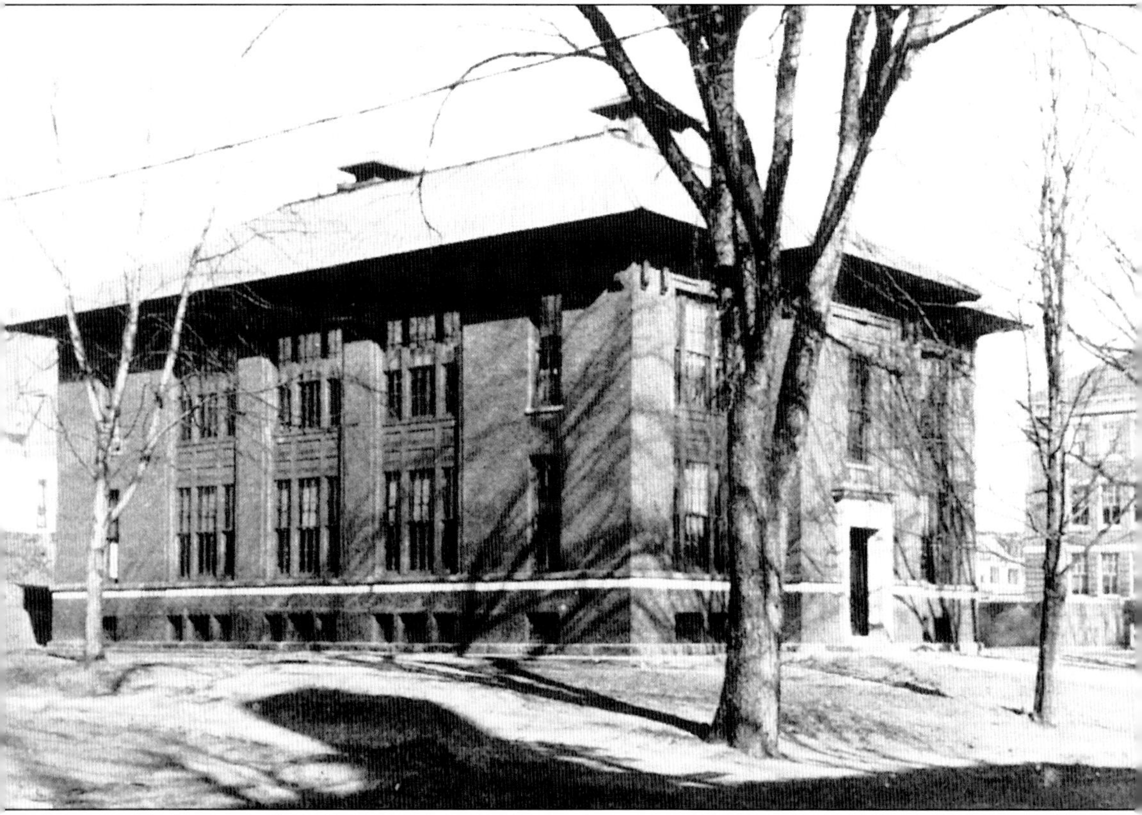

Pupils living in the village section of town in the 1830s embarked upon an association with the precursors of what is now Plymouth State College. Both school facilities and instruction lasted for the most part over a period of 140 years. The earlier years saw the pupils attending school in buildings housing Holmes Academy and later its successor, Plymouth Normal School. In 1910, the village students acquired their own exclusive home in the Model School at the corner of Summer and School Streets. The name resulted from the fact that the supervising teachers were also Normal School faculty members. Also, senior class members of the Normal School were student teachers.

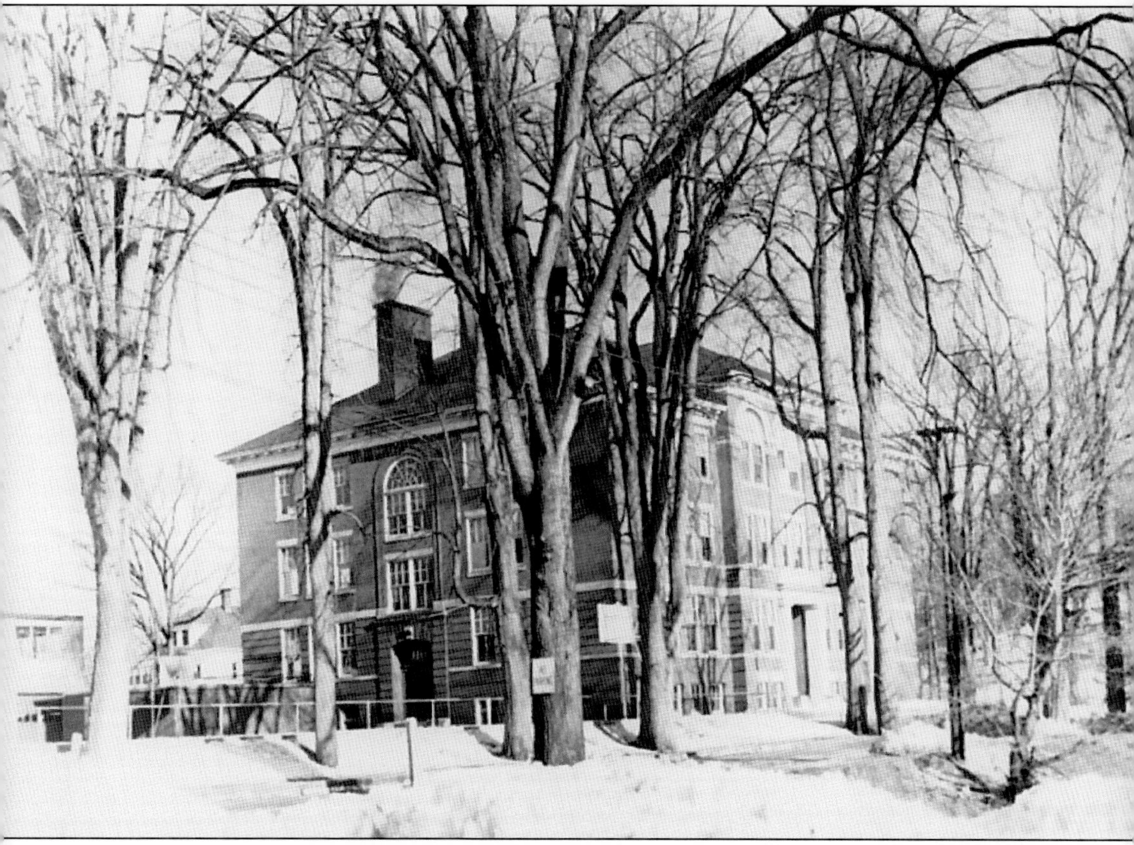

The first high school was established in 1883 and met in Normal School facilities and in a downtown business block until 1903. Then it acquired its own building at the corner of Summer and High Streets. The original building was lost to fire in 1914. It was replaced by a three-story structure that was sold to Plymouth State College in 1970, when all schools were moved to the new regional facilities.

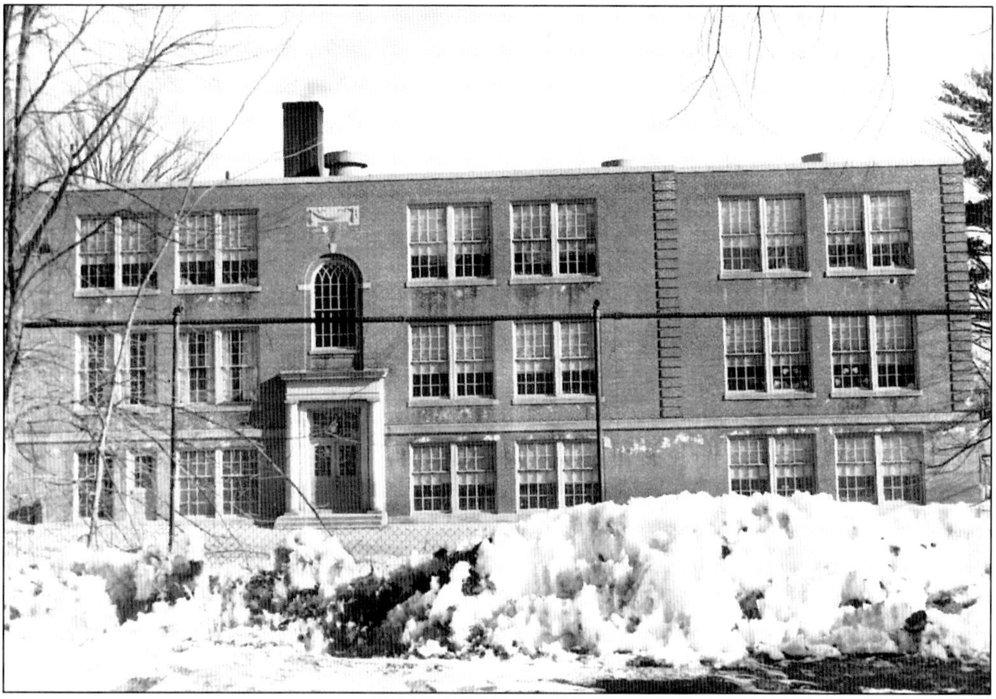

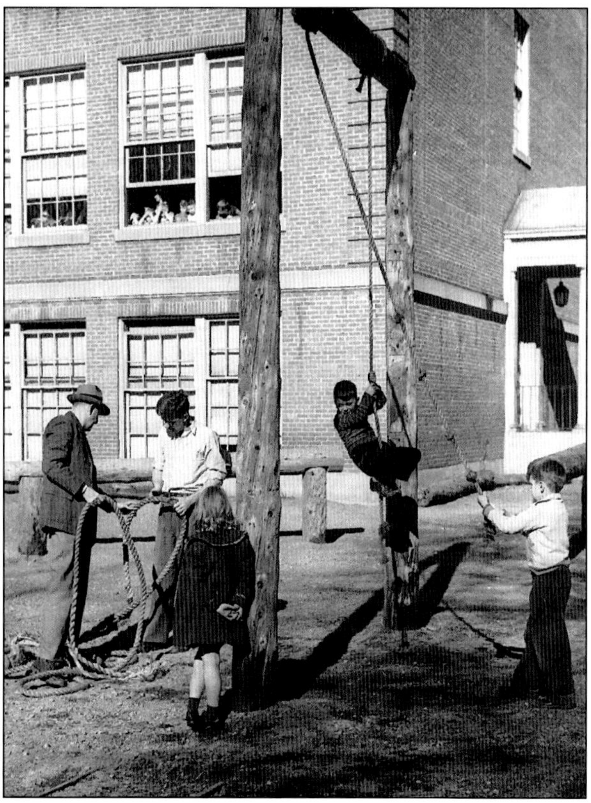

During the Depression, with generous assistance of federal financial aid, Plymouth consolidated its elementary schools into a single, new facility. It was dedicated in 1939 opposite the high school on Summer Street. The Model School was closed, and in 1941, so too were the four remaining district schools. Increased enrollment necessitated the reopening of the Model School in 1950. Both buildings were subsequently purchased by Plymouth State College when the area schools were regionalized.

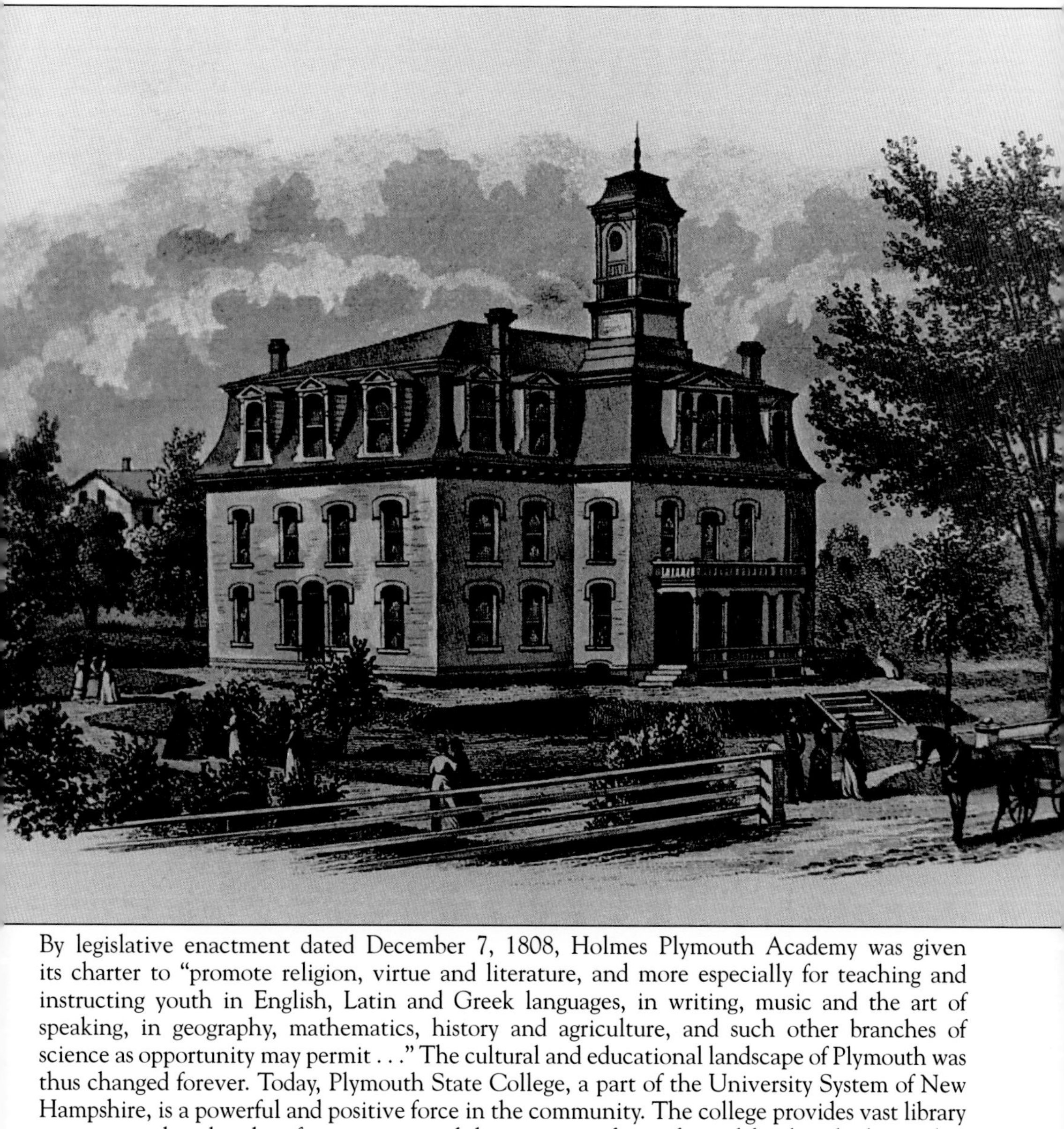

By legislative enactment dated December 7, 1808, Holmes Plymouth Academy was given its charter to "promote religion, virtue and literature, and more especially for teaching and instructing youth in English, Latin and Greek languages, in writing, music and the art of speaking, in geography, mathematics, history and agriculture, and such other branches of science as opportunity may permit . . ." The cultural and educational landscape of Plymouth was thus changed forever. Today, Plymouth State College, a part of the University System of New Hampshire, is a powerful and positive force in the community. The college provides vast library resources, cultural and performing arts, and the presence of an informed faculty which enriches the lives of all persons within its reach, but most particularly, the citizens of Plymouth.

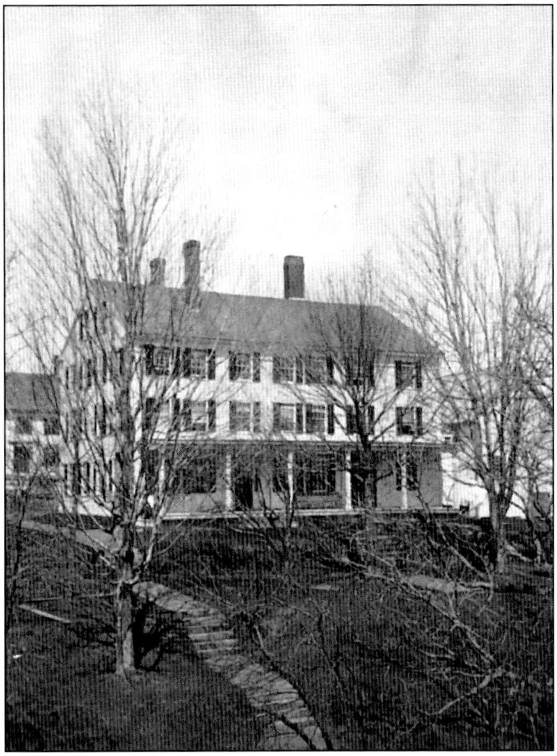

Some of the students who received instruction at Holmes Academy were housed in the boardinghouse, which was located on the present site of Rounds Hall.

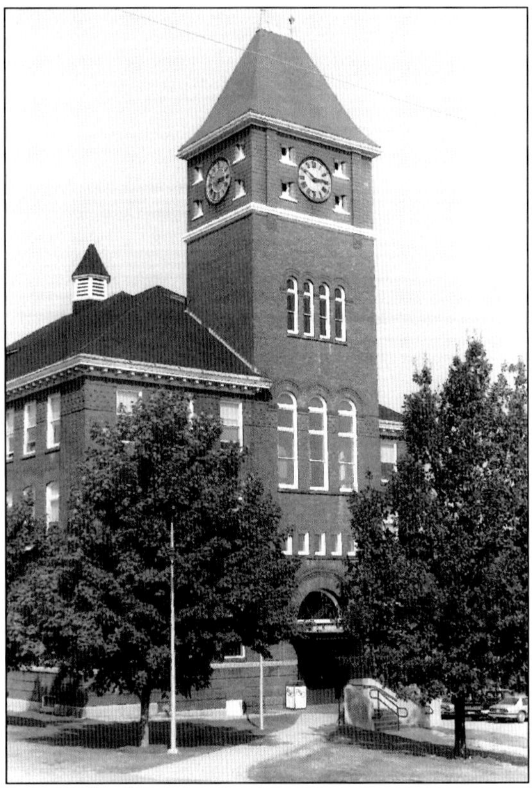

The influence of Plymouth State College has, since 1891, been identified by the commanding presence of Rounds Hall. It overlooks the town from its site at the corner of Summer and Court Streets and contains the so-called "Town Clock."

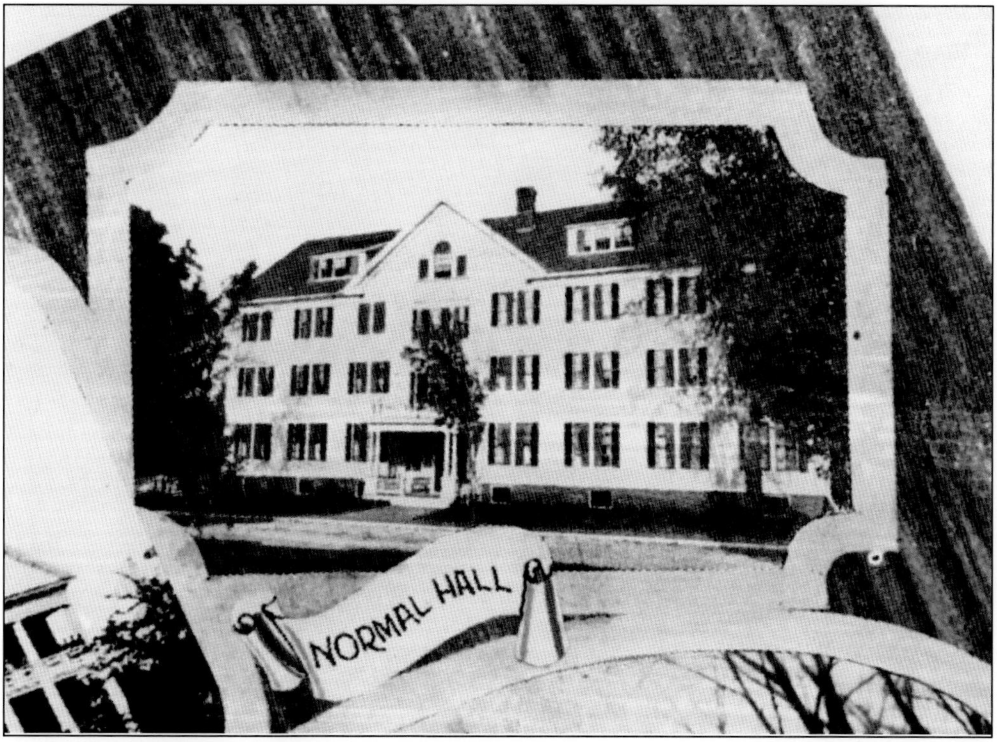

Under the vigorous leadership of Plymouth Normal School president Charles Collins Rounds, the legislature was required to provide additional housing for the college, including Normal Hall. It was constructed in the early 1880s on a site south of School Street and between Summer Street and Highland Avenue. It was renovated and enlarged in 1905; after the 1909 fire, which destroyed the second Pemigewasset Hotel, it was physically moved south across Highland Street to be incorporated as the East Wing of the new Pemigewasset Hotel.

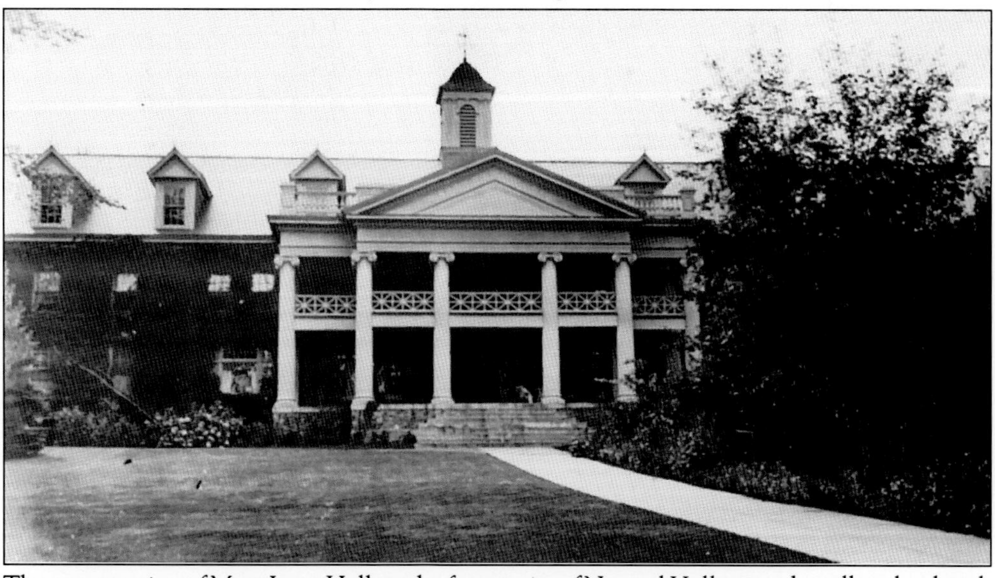

The construction of Mary Lyon Hall on the former site of Normal Hall created a college landmark second only to Rounds Hall as a statement of the college presence in the community.

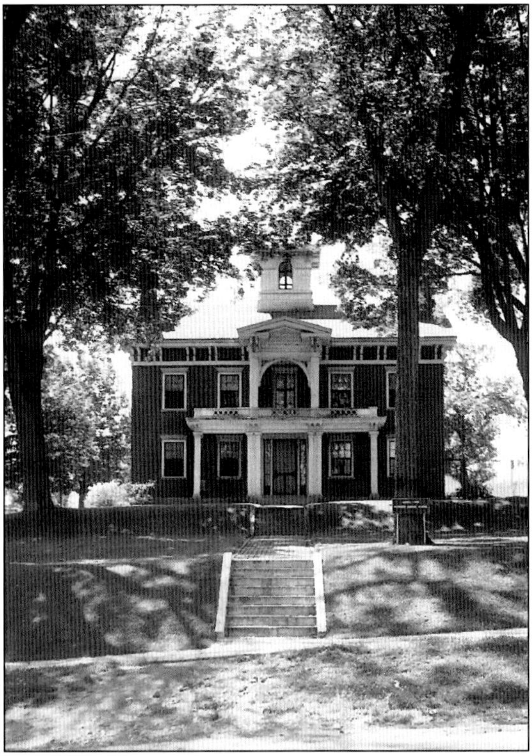

Moor Russell, a veteran of the Battle of Bunker Hill, married a Plymouth woman, Elizabeth Webster, and prospered as a land surveyor and tradesman. The Russells enlarged their home on Highland Street in 1825 with this brick addition. It still stands, minus its cupola and upper porch, and now houses administrative offices of Plymouth State College.

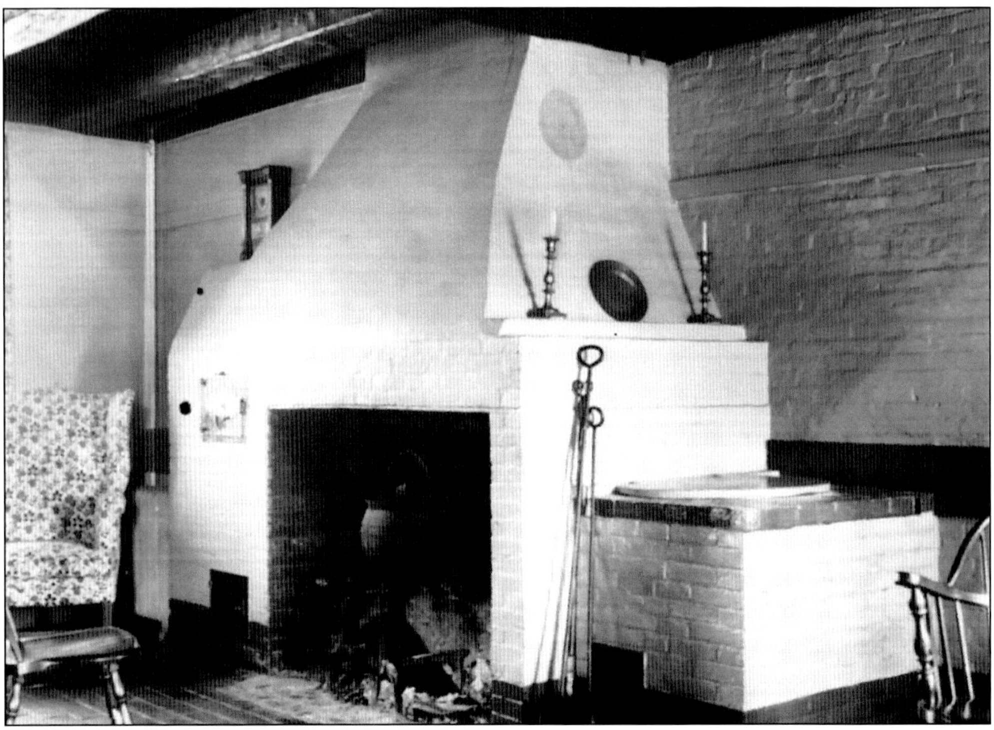

Long a point of particular interest in Russell House, as it is now known, has been the original 1797 kitchen with its Rumford fireplace and hot-water reservoir, both of which remain intact.

Six

Public Buildings

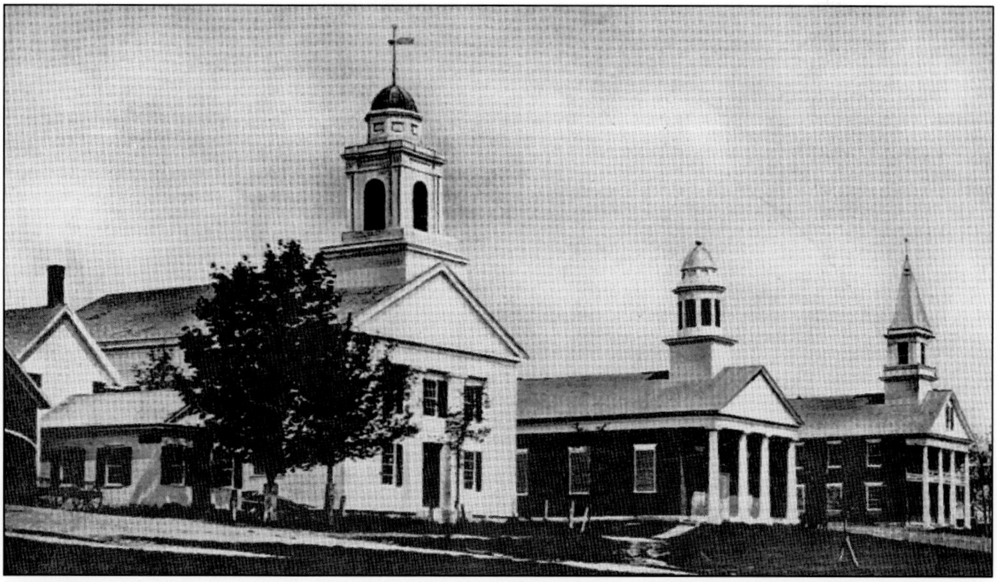

In 1855, the facades of three imposing buildings dominated downtown Plymouth. They were the Congregational church, the Grafton County Court House of 1823, and the Holmes Academy Building.

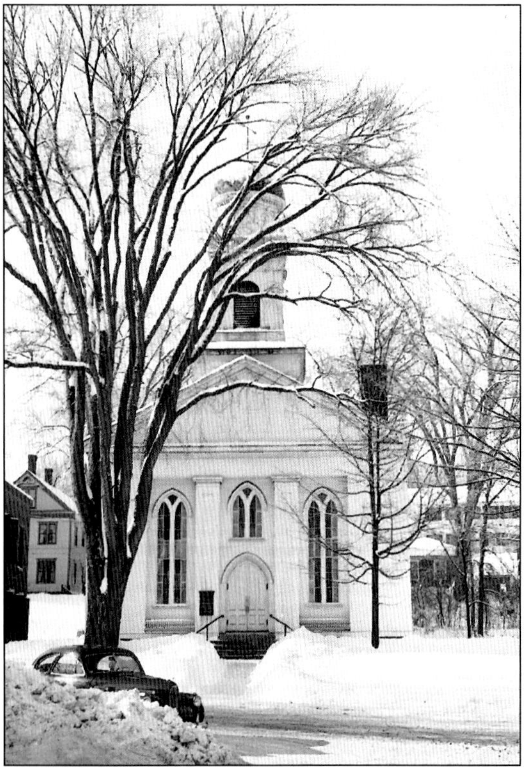

Built as the third meetinghouse of the Congregational Church, this building was erected in 1836 and dedicated in December of that year. Open to other groups for many of its early years, this gracious edifice sited on the east side of the Common became a familiar and admired landmark of downtown Plymouth. Its loss to the disastrous fire of 1983 was felt by many in the Plymouth area.

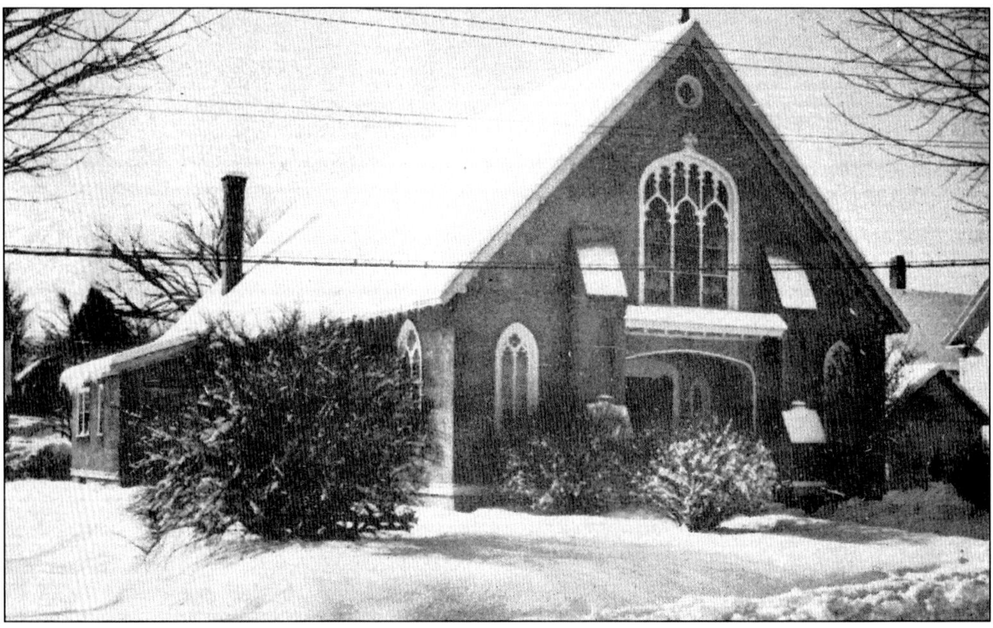

Having been a mission of Ashland since 1904, the St. Matthews Parish congregation expanded and outgrew its borrowed accommodations in the Universalist church, which had closed. The parish purchased land on School Street and erected its own edifice, which was dedicated October 12, 1912, by Bishop Georges Albert Guertin. It remains today serving the Catholic community.

In 1943, the second Methodist Church meetinghouse in Plymouth, built in 1872, was demolished in a spectacular and infamous blaze. The fire also destroyed the Kidder Block next door and forever changed the look of Plymouth's Main Street.

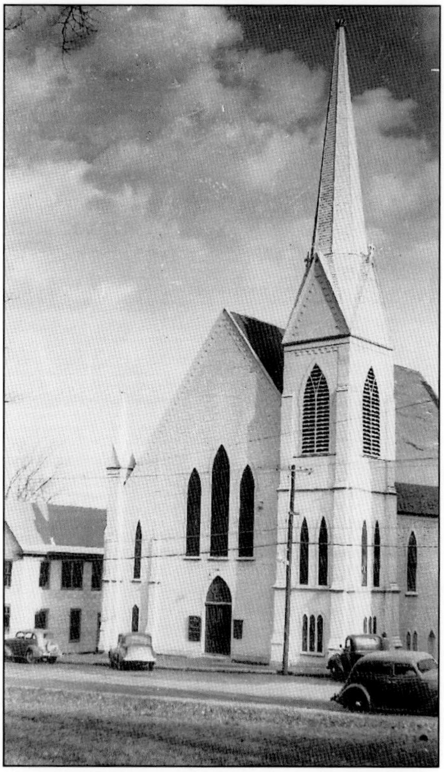

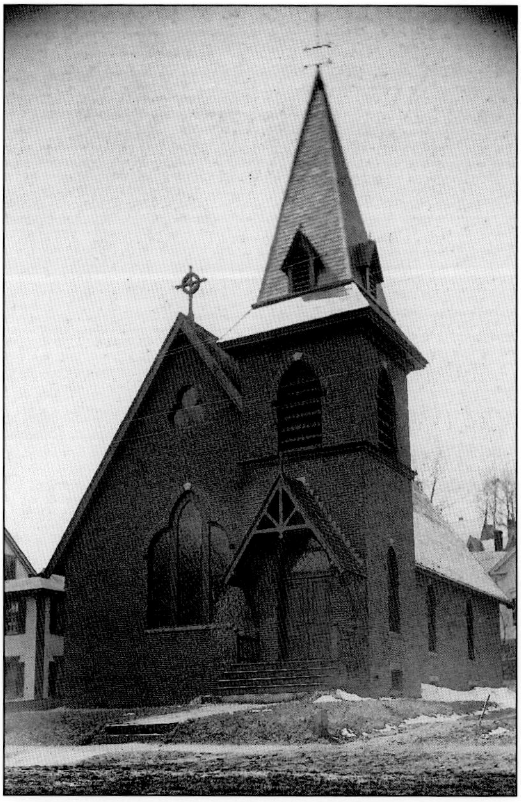

For many years, those from Plymouth of the Episcopal faith attended services at the Holy Cross Chapel of Holderness School for Boys. With a growing enrollment at the school, the chapel became overcrowded and the people of Plymouth began attending the Ashland Episcopal Church. Wishing to maintain their own church, they purchased the Universalist church building on North Main Street and established the Church of the Holy Spirit.

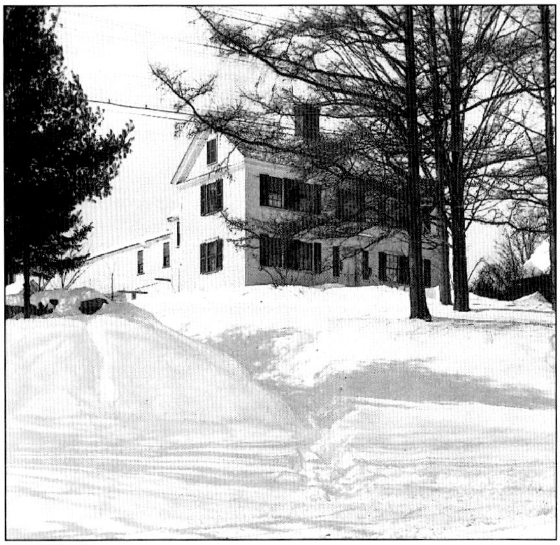

The first Emily Balch Cottage hospital was established in 1899 in this residence, which stood at 37 Highland Street. It is the present site of Belknap Hall of Plymouth State College. The hospital struggled on for several years with one trained nurse and donations of the generous citizens of Plymouth.

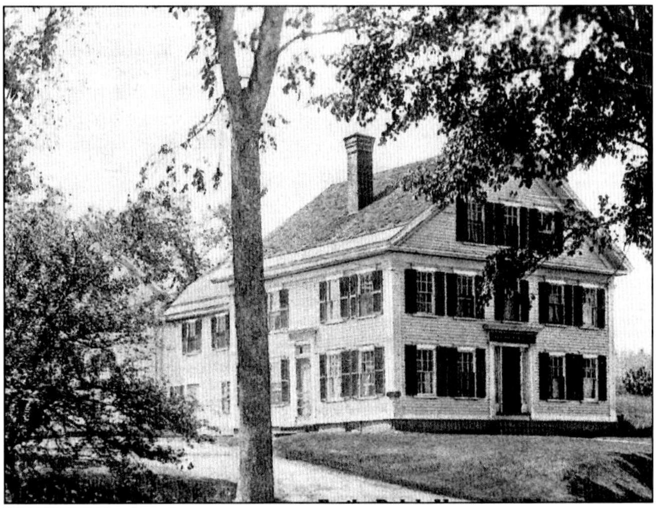

In 1909, the Emily Balch Cottage Hospital Association purchased the private hospital of Dr. Ernest L. Bell at 65 Highland Street, which opened in 1904. Only seven years later, after starting a successful training school for nurses and affording the community better services, the building was severely damaged by fire, forcing the closing of the facility.

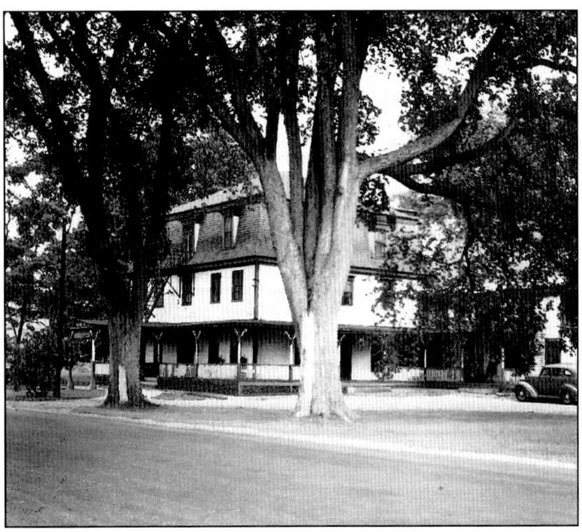

At a special town meeting in August of 1919, the sum of $3,500 was approved for the establishment of a third hospital. It was the proviso that the name be the Emily Balch and Soldiers and Sailors Memorial Hospital in recognition of all who had served in World War I. With the purchase of the Schofield property at the Campton town line near Livermore Falls, and with private donations and community effort, the hospital opened in 1920. It served the area for the next three decades, until the construction of the Speare Memorial Hospital in 1951.

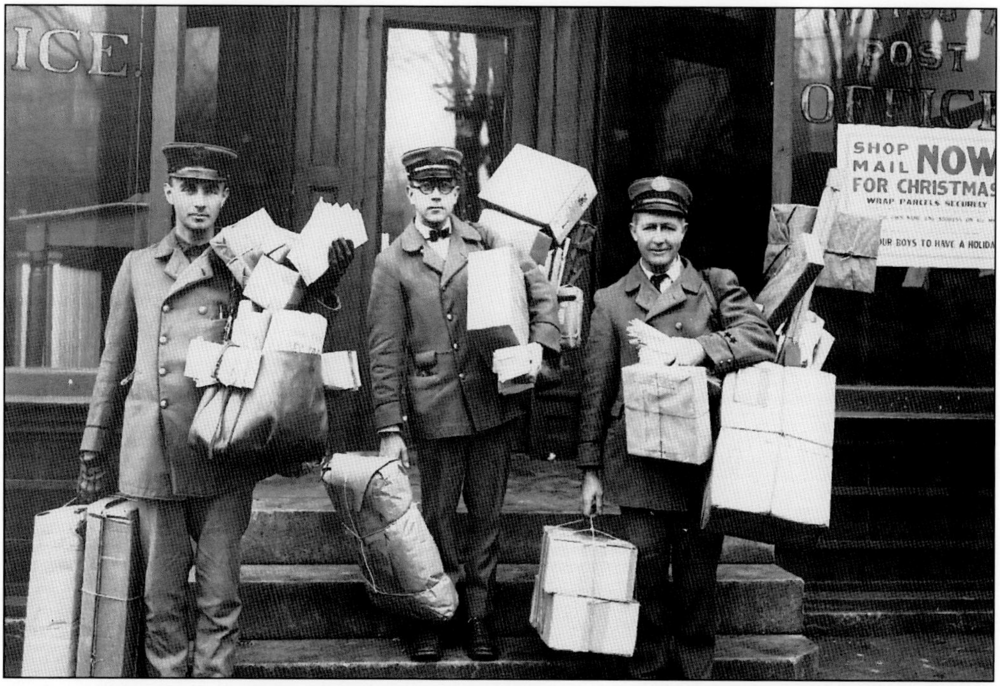

In the 1920s, the post office was located in the Kidder Block on Main Street. Here Harold Sherburn, Harold Freeman, and Edmund Shanahan are ready to make their rounds.

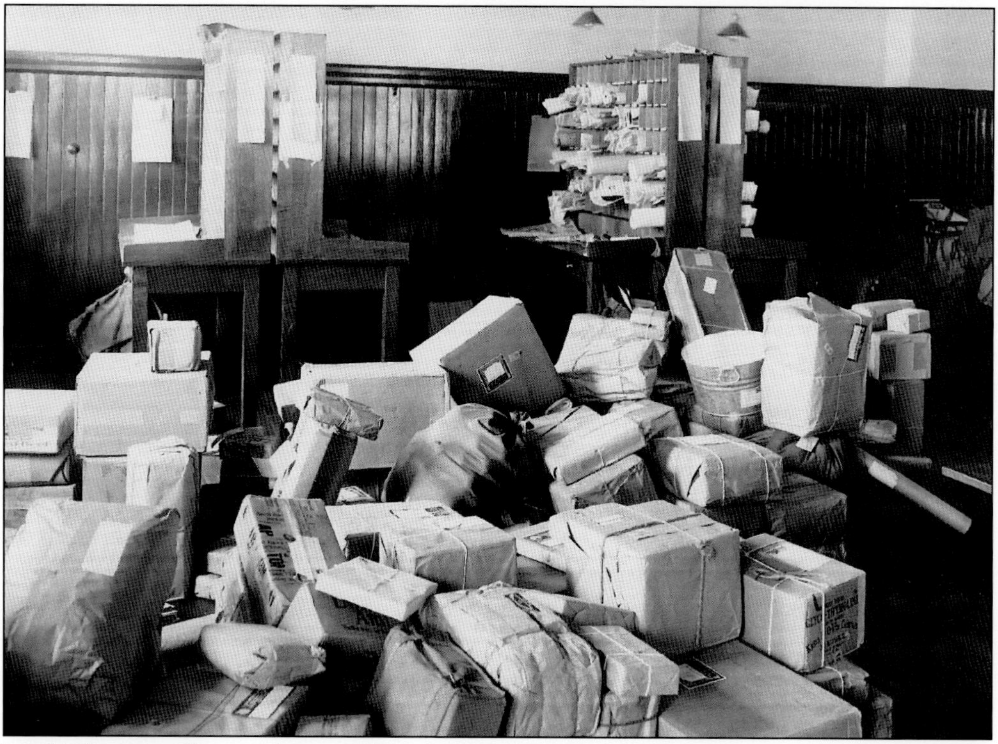

Inside the post office, packages and mail await their final destinations. Too bad we can't read some of the address labels.

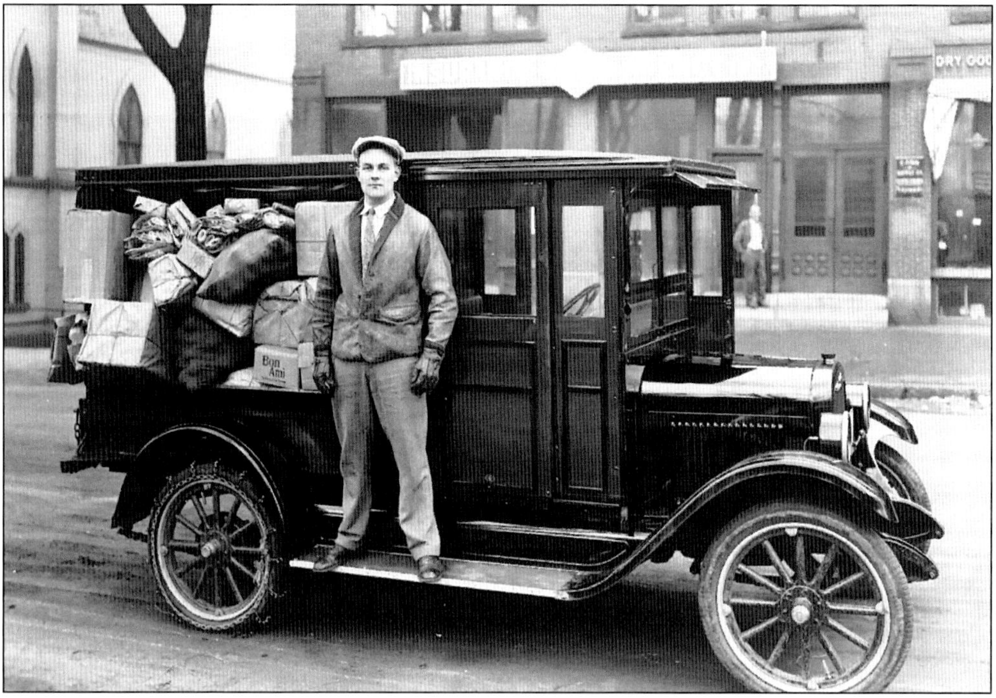

For parcel post deliveries, a truck was rented from William Dearborn for 50¢ an hour. Mac Keniston prepares to head out onto the roads of Plymouth.

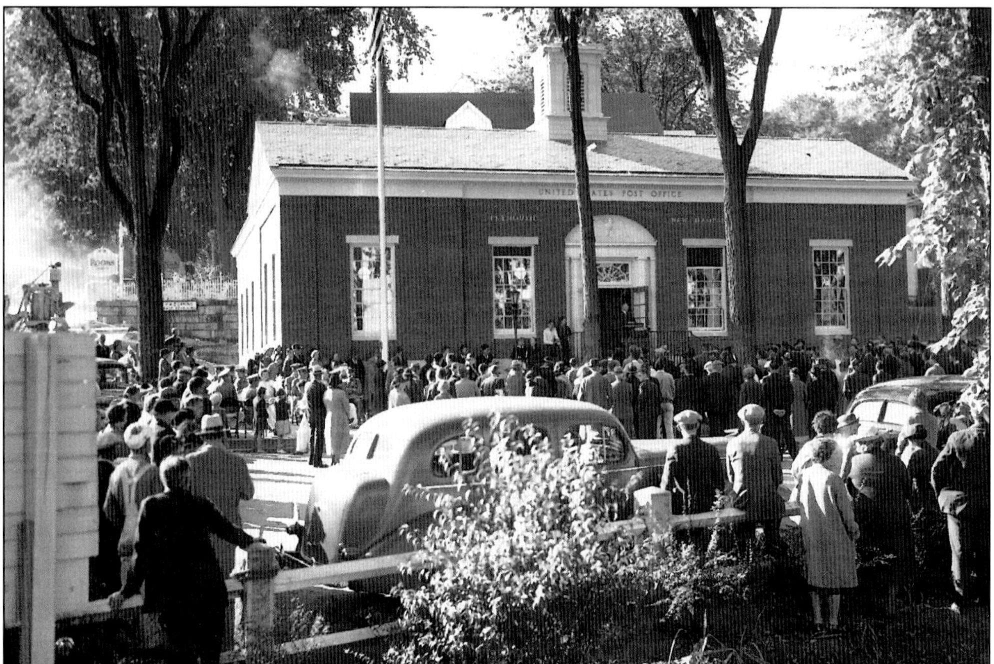

The new post office was built on the site of the "Old Brick" at the corner of Highland Street opposite the Common. A large crowd assembled for the dedication ceremonies on October 4, 1937.

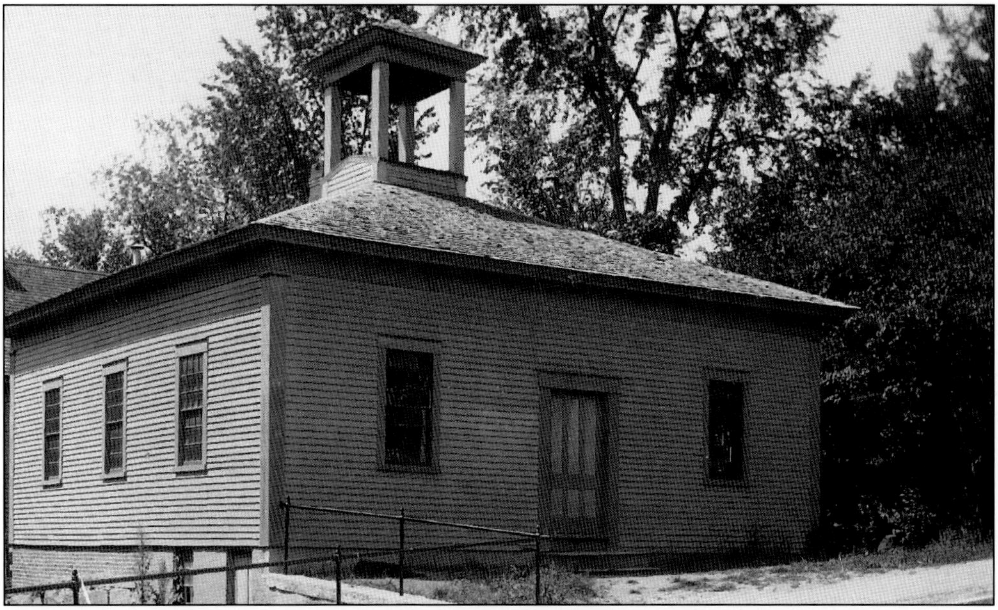

This familiar building, built as the first county courthouse in Plymouth in 1774, was where Daniel Webster pled his first case in 1806. It has gone from Main Street to Russell Street to South Main and then to its current location on Court Street. It has served as a schoolhouse, a paint shop, a wheelwright's shop, and as the town library. Today it is the museum of the Plymouth Historical Society and is owned by the Young Ladies Library Association.

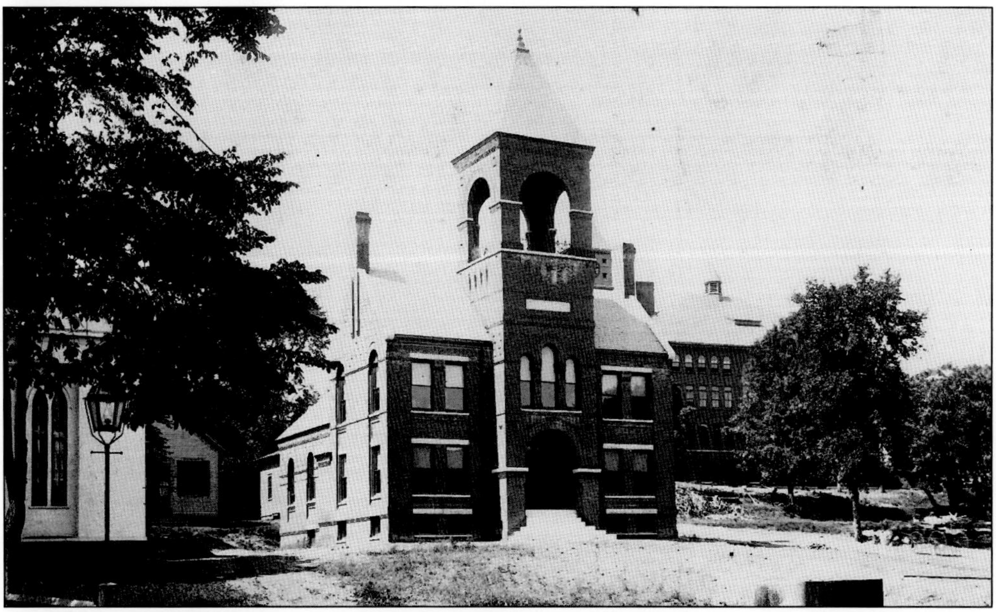

In 1890, the third county courthouse was erected on the site of its deteriorating predecessor and served Grafton County until a new county facility was built in Woodsville in 1969. The Plymouth selectmen's offices, town offices, and police department subsequently moved into the former county courthouse with the Plymouth District Court. With the building of a new district court facility on Green Street, the century-old building was beautifully remodeled in 1996 and is now the Plymouth Town Hall.

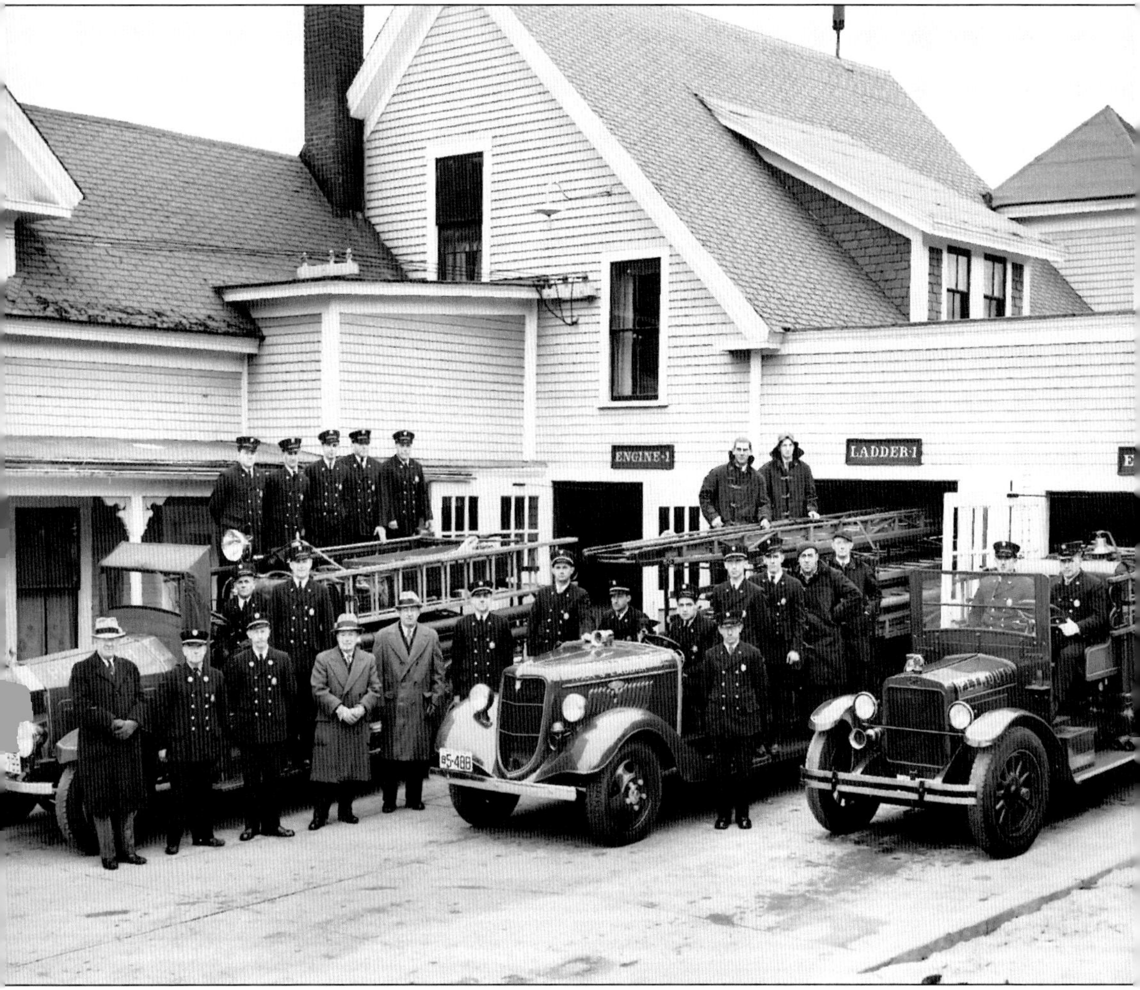

The Plymouth Fire Department began in 1831 as the Village Fire Precinct and in 1881 it became the Plymouth Aqueduct and Water Company. At that time James Fogg Langdon devised a system of waterworks for fire and domestic purposes. His efforts were in response to the deaths, among others, of his daughter-in-law and grandson from an epidemic of typhoid fever in 1880. The corporation was dissolved in 1889 and the Plymouth Village Fire District took over. In 1937, the firehouse was located at 42 Highland Street on the same site that the current station was built in 1969.

Seven

FIRE, FLOOD, AND WIND

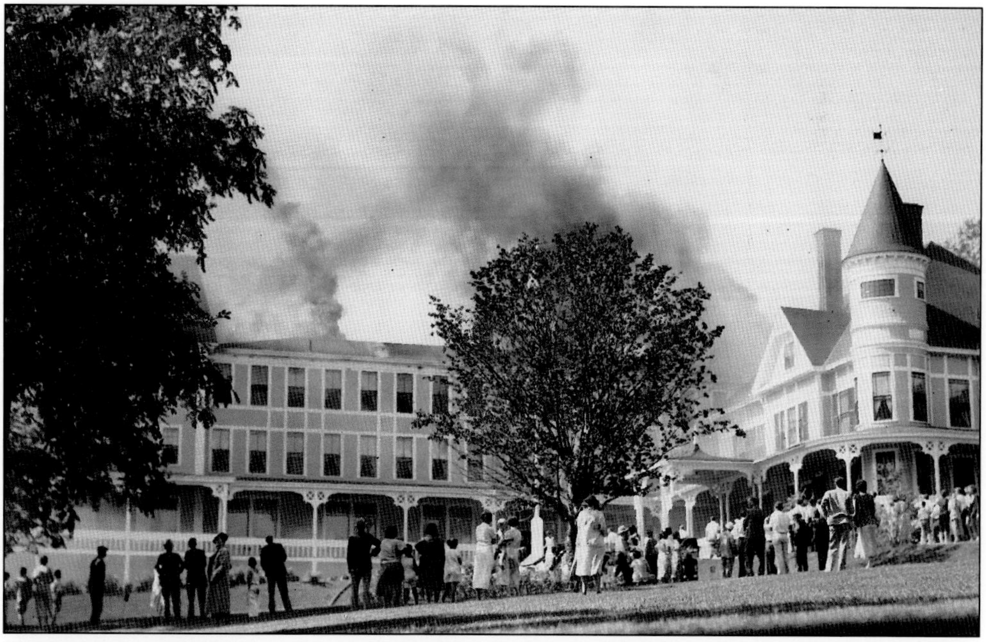

Fire had taken the first two Pemigewasset Hotels, for which Plymouth was well known, and in 1934 it threatened to take the third of the famous hostelries. Response by the fire department was rapid and the battle was won. After repairs were made, the hotel was quickly back in business and it retained its status and popularity until 1958, when it was razed.

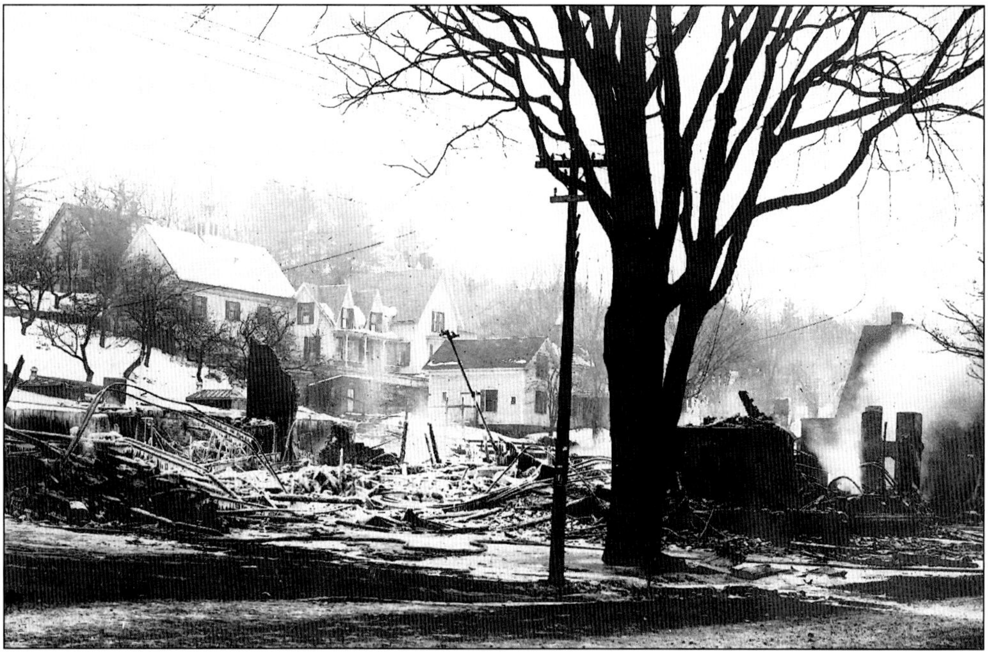

Fire has taken its toll in Plymouth over the years, leaving behind rubble and toil. In 1911, the large wooden structure of the D&M factory on North Main Street was totally burned, leaving only smoking debris and putting many people out of work. A three-story brick building was immediately erected on the same site and even more workers found employment there.

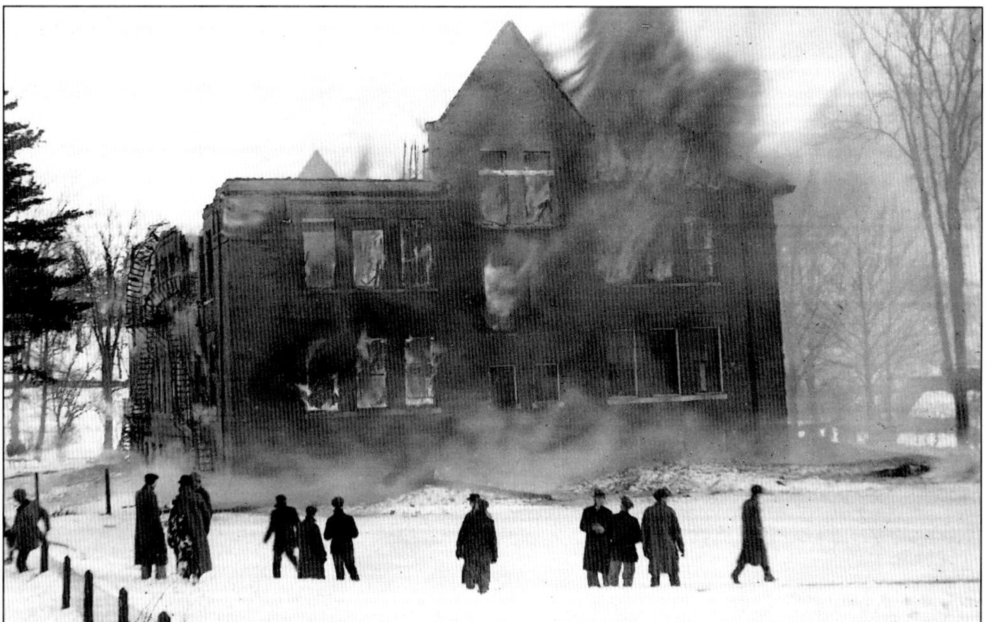

A fire on a cold morning in 1913 soon went out of control, destroying the Plymouth High School building at Summer and High Streets. The school was built in 1904. The Town immediately appropriated funds for a larger facility on the same site, which remained for more than a half century.

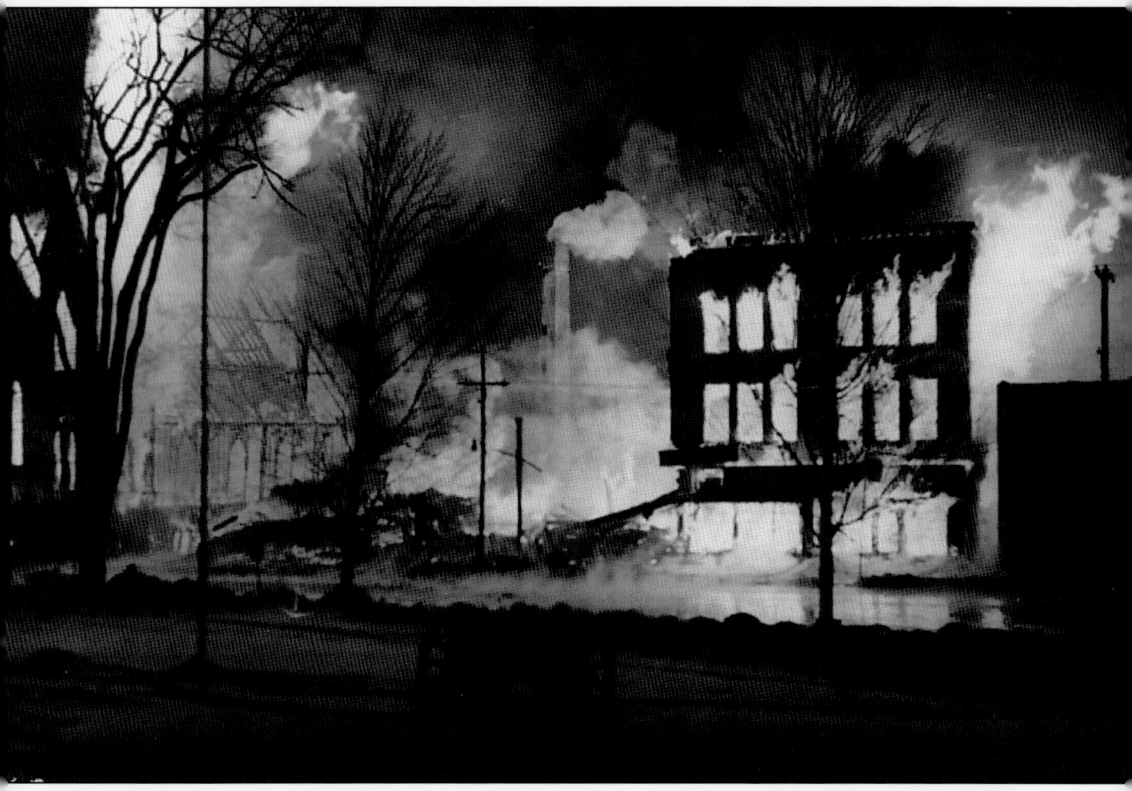

Perhaps Plymouth's most well-known fire was the inferno in 1943, which consumed the Kidder Block and the Methodist church on Main Street. Two landmarks were gone, but the owner of the Kidder Block, William O'Brien, rebuilt a modern structure in 1946 and new businesses were soon flourishing. These included O'Brien's Department Store, Geyer's Pharmacy, and Fracher's Hardware.

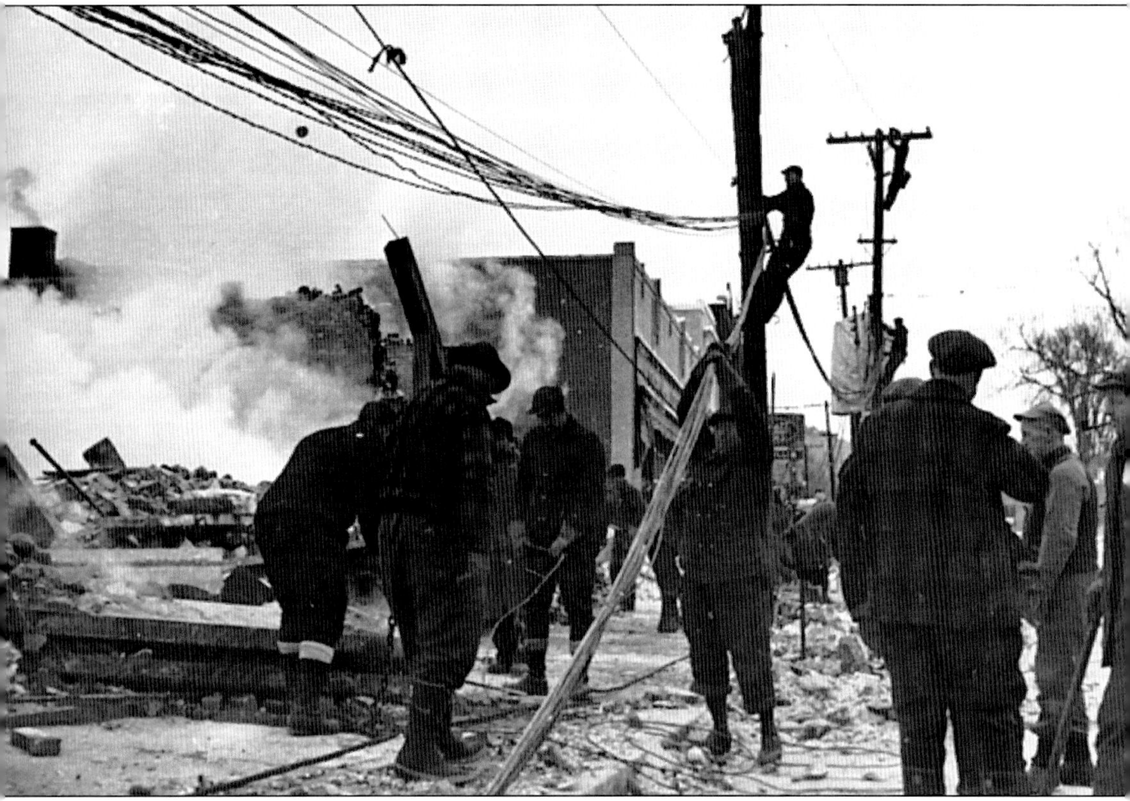

The morning after the disastrous fire, the wreckage still threw up plenty of smoke and heat as people gathered to begin the cleaning-up process.

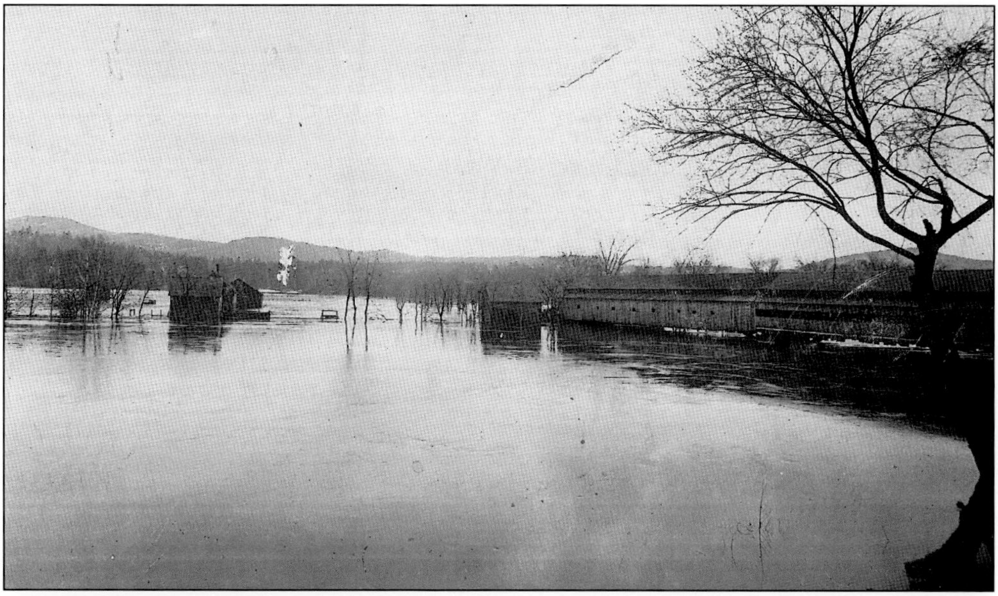

Located at the point where the Baker River flows into the Pemigewasset, the town of Plymouth is frequently the scene of high water and flooding. This scene from April 1895 shows Pont Lafayette, the old covered bridge from Plymouth to the Holderness Intervale, barely above the crest of flood waters which extend across the flats.

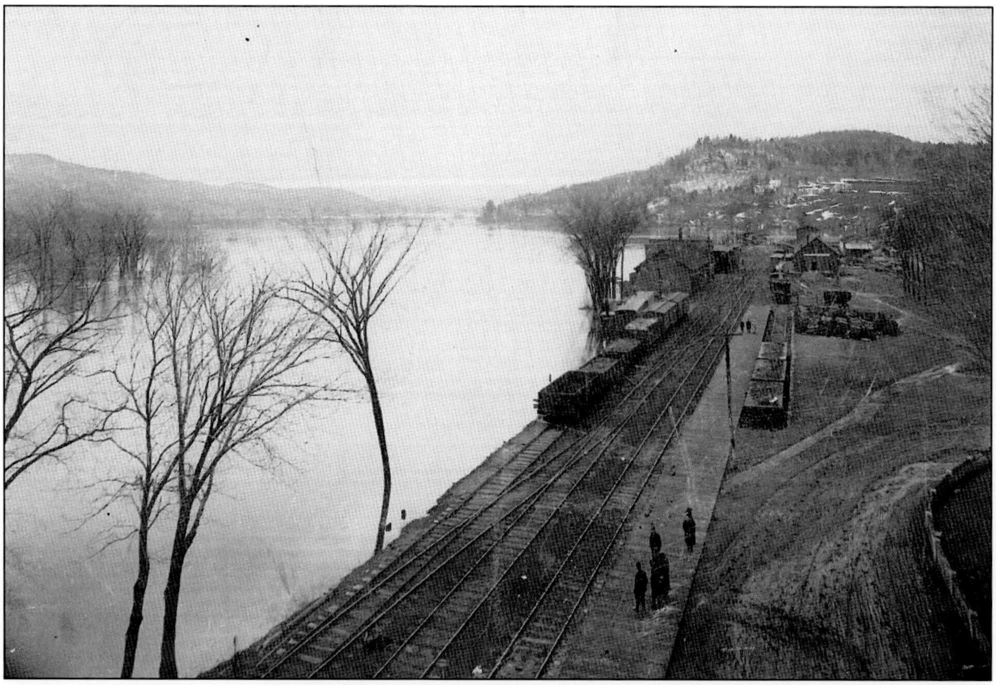

The April 1895 flood reached the very edge of the railway yards, but did not go over the tracks.

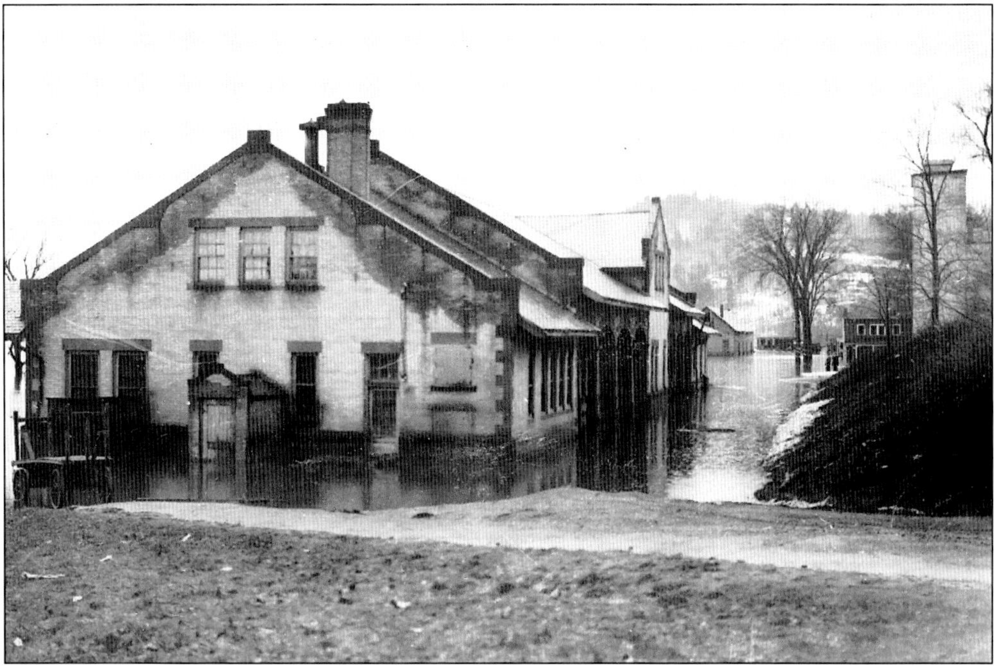

In 1936, the river rose well over its banks and the railroad tracks, and the station itself was in 2 feet of water.

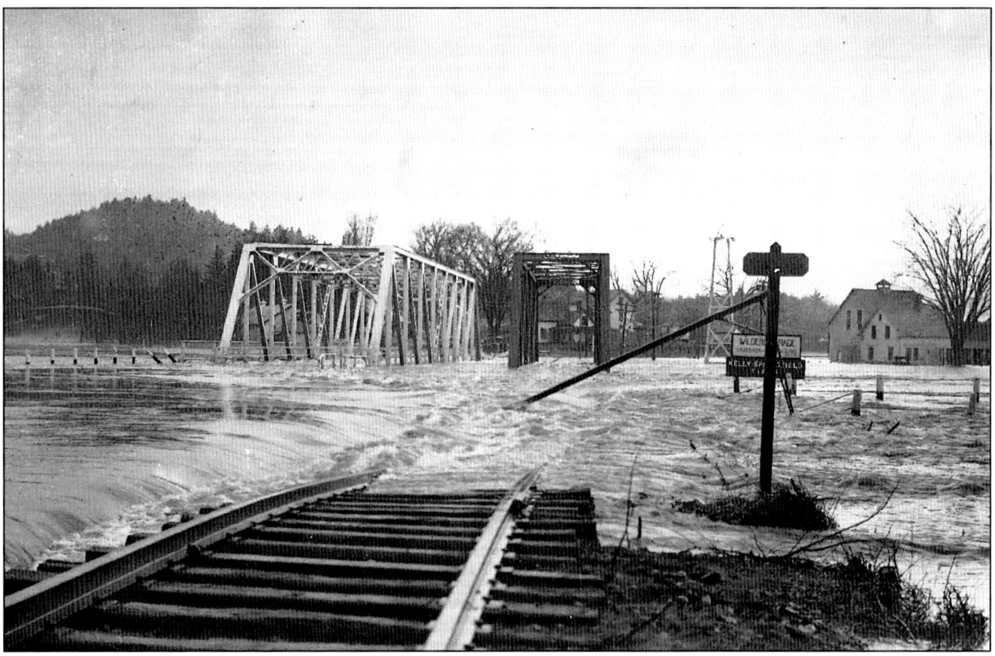

At the confluence of the two rivers just north of town, the 1936 floodwaters surged over Route 3 and the railroad bed, causing severe washouts and undermining the bridges. The view shown here is looking north. Repairs were quickly made and both spans are still in service today.

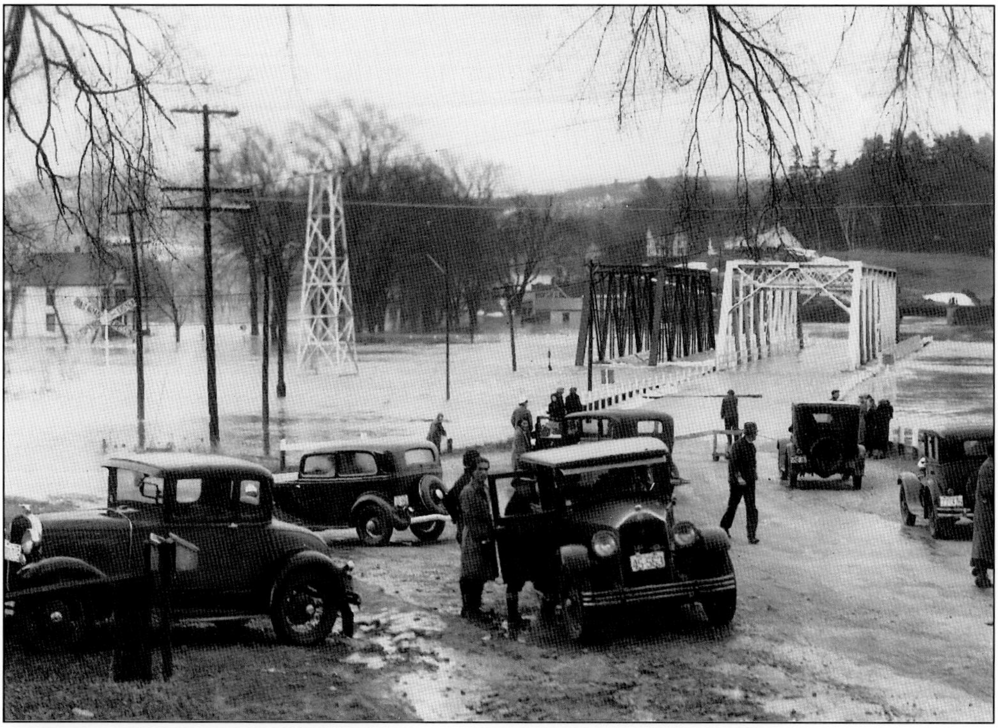

Looking south from Peg Mill Hill, the scene was one of fascination and frustration as the March 1936 flood isolated the town of Plymouth.

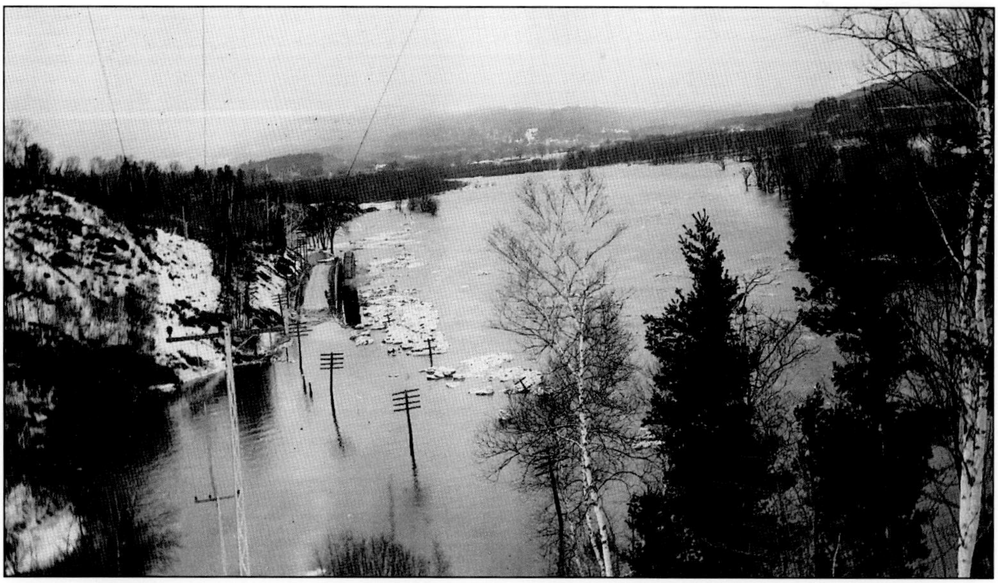

South of Plymouth, the flood cut off Route 3 and the B&M railroad tracks, marooning the steam engine *Alouette* before it could make its escape.

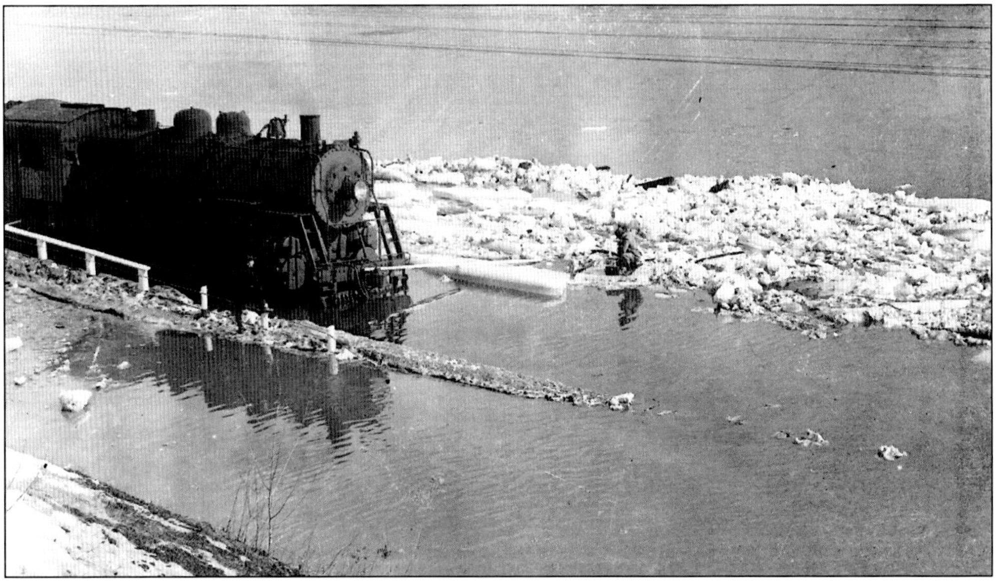

Receding waters left huge cakes of ice and downed power lines, which kept the *Alouette* stranded while crews worked to clear the highway and railway.

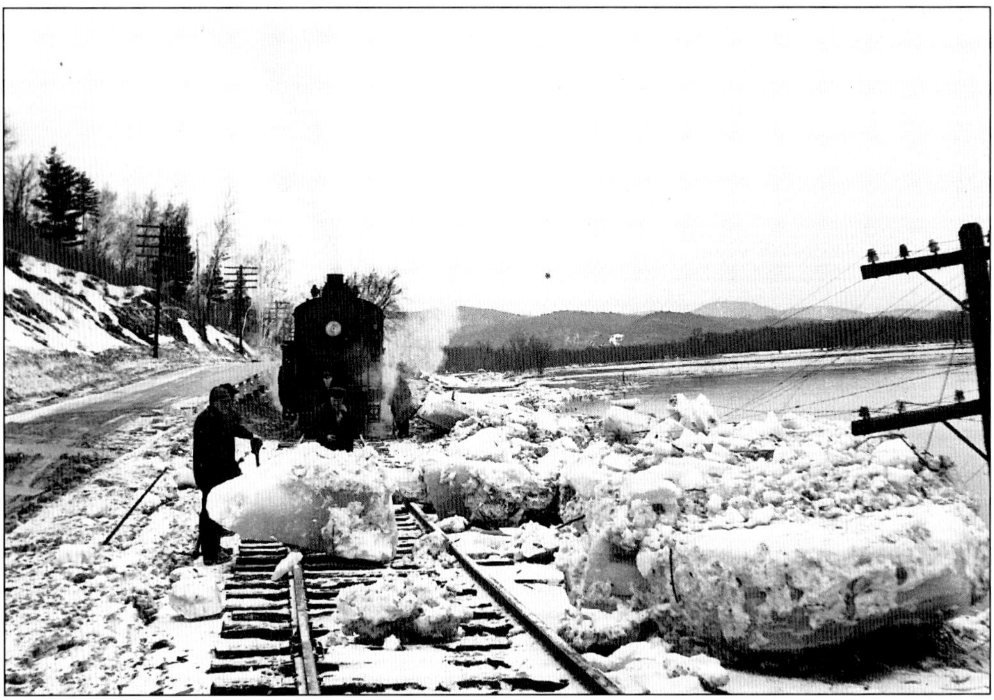

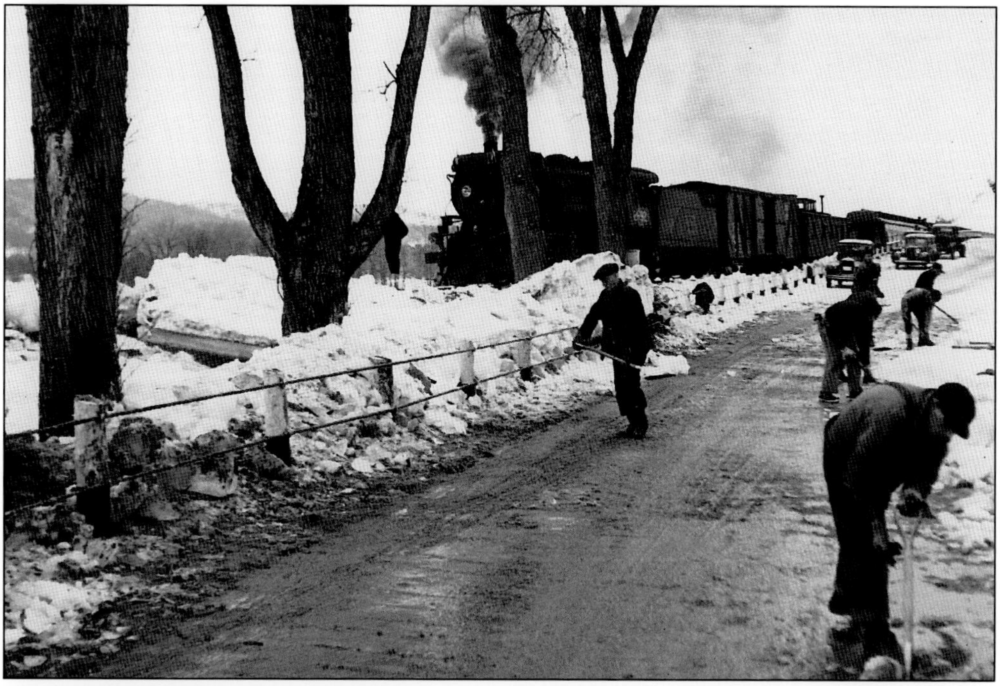

It was finally decided to back another engine to the idled train and tow it back to the Plymouth station while clean-up work continued.

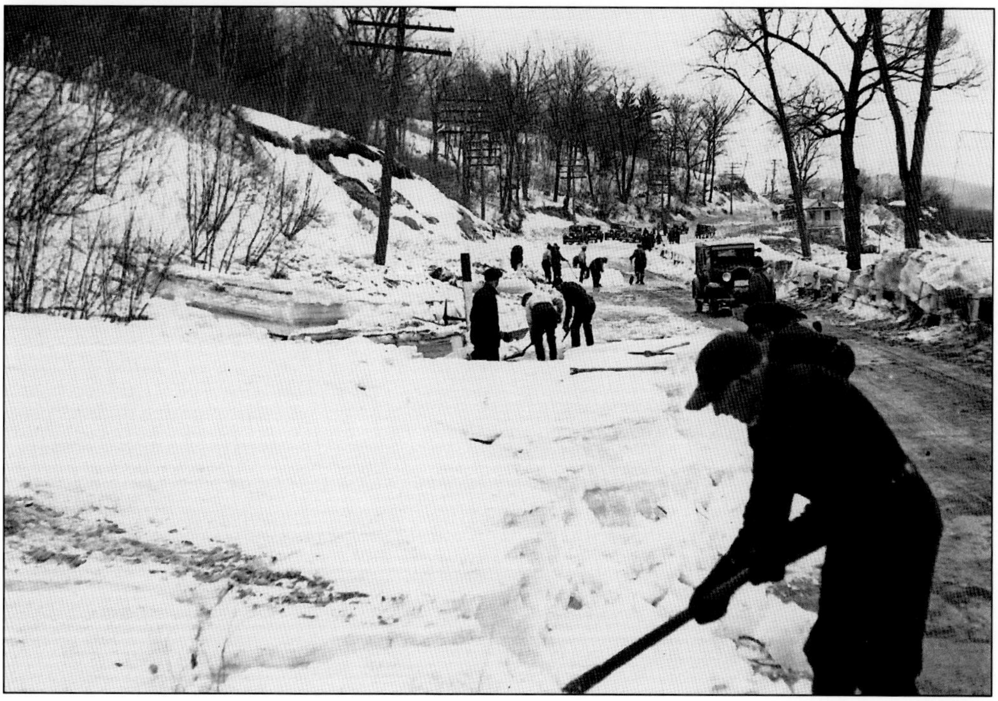

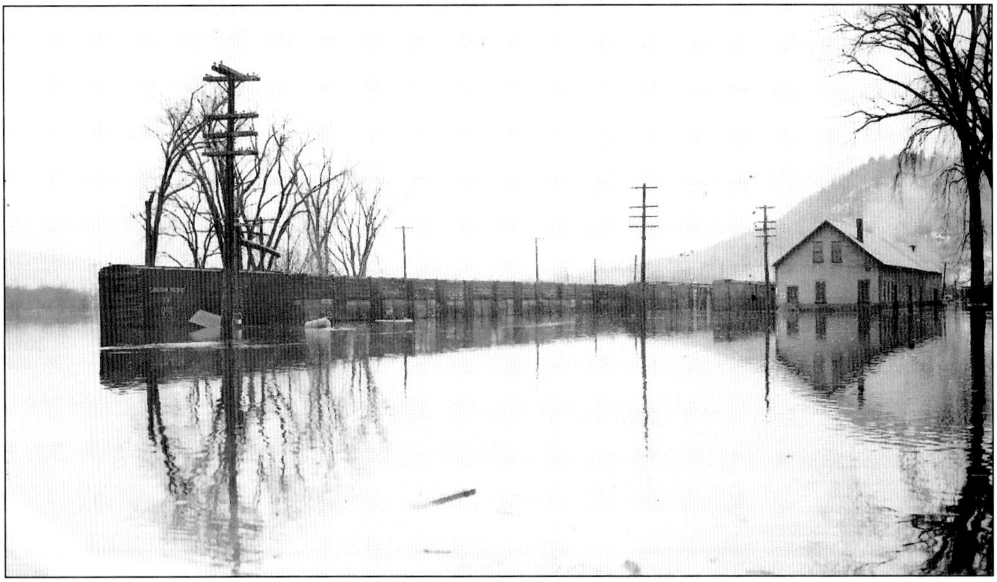

At the railyards, a line of freight cars were caught by the floodwaters. One car contained lime, which ignited when it made contact with the water. Firefighters working from boats saved the other cars from being destroyed.

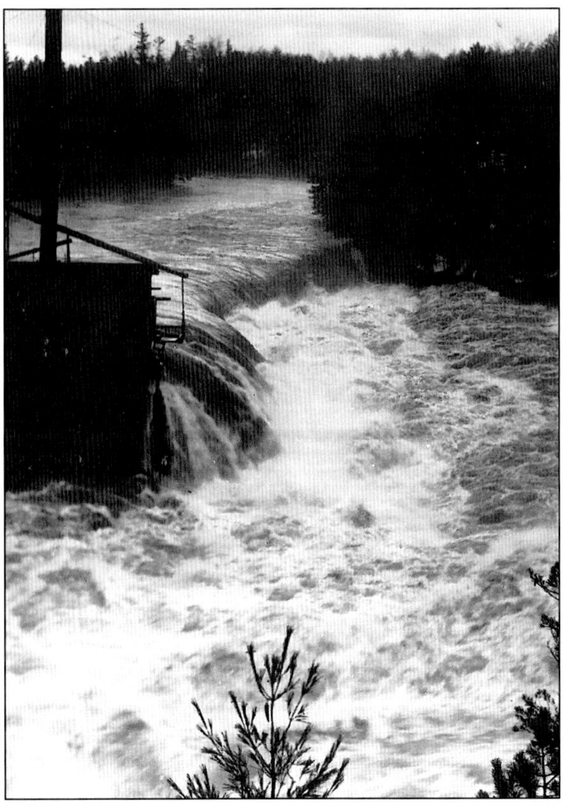

This view of Livermore Falls during the 1936 flood, just above the Campton town line north of Plymouth, shows the power which once was harnessed to operate the mills at this site.

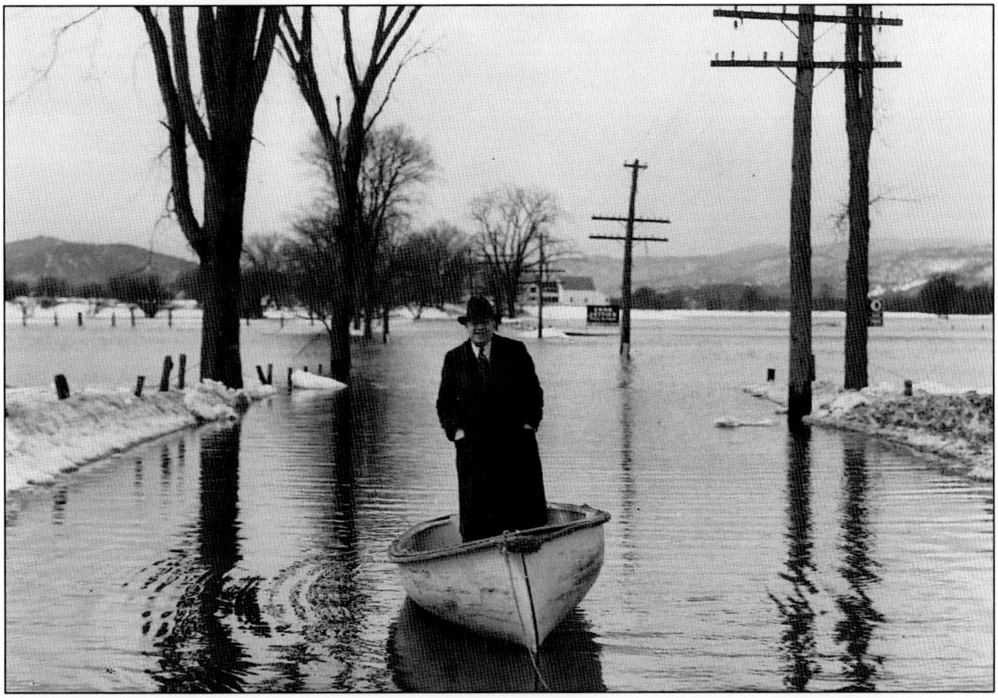

West of Plymouth on Route 25, where Tenney Mountain Highway now runs, boats were the preferred mode of transportation when the waters of the Baker River spread over the fields of "Clarkland" in 1936. Two of George Clark's barnyard residents—one pig and one duck—found their own Mt. Ararat in their usually tranquil surroundings.

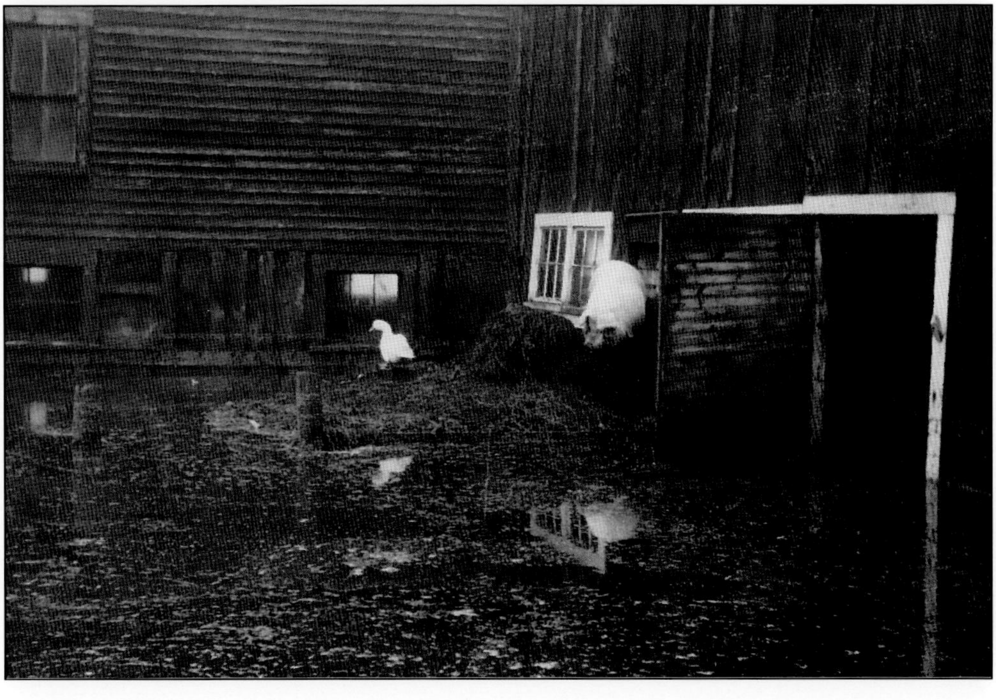

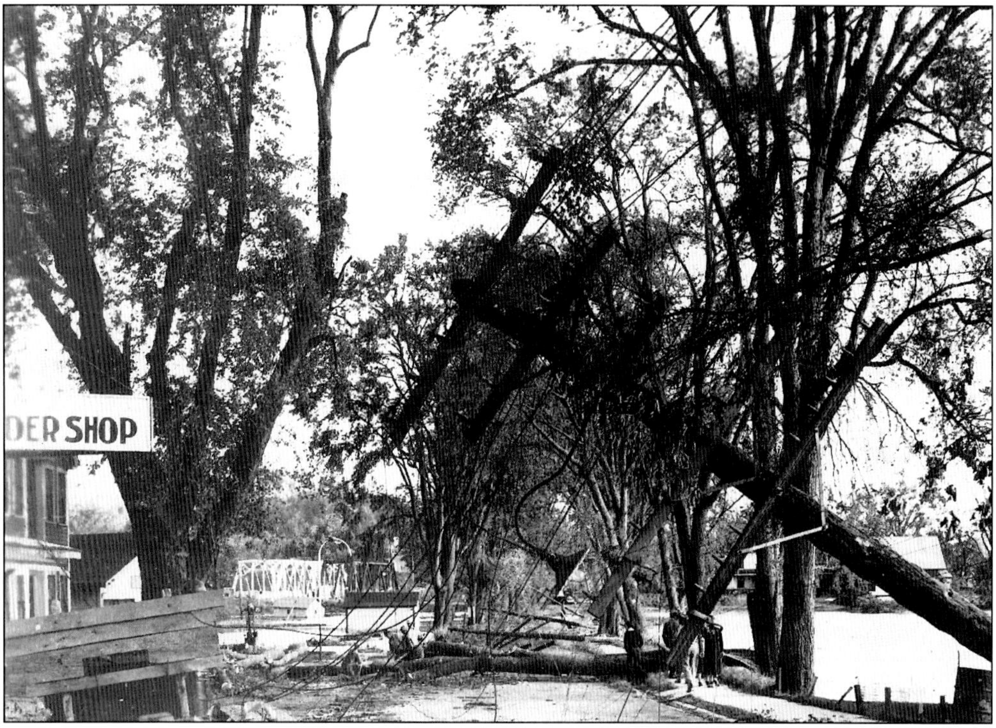

This view of downtown showing the Methodist church, the Record office, and the Sargent Block documents the aftermath of the hurricane which so devastated the town.

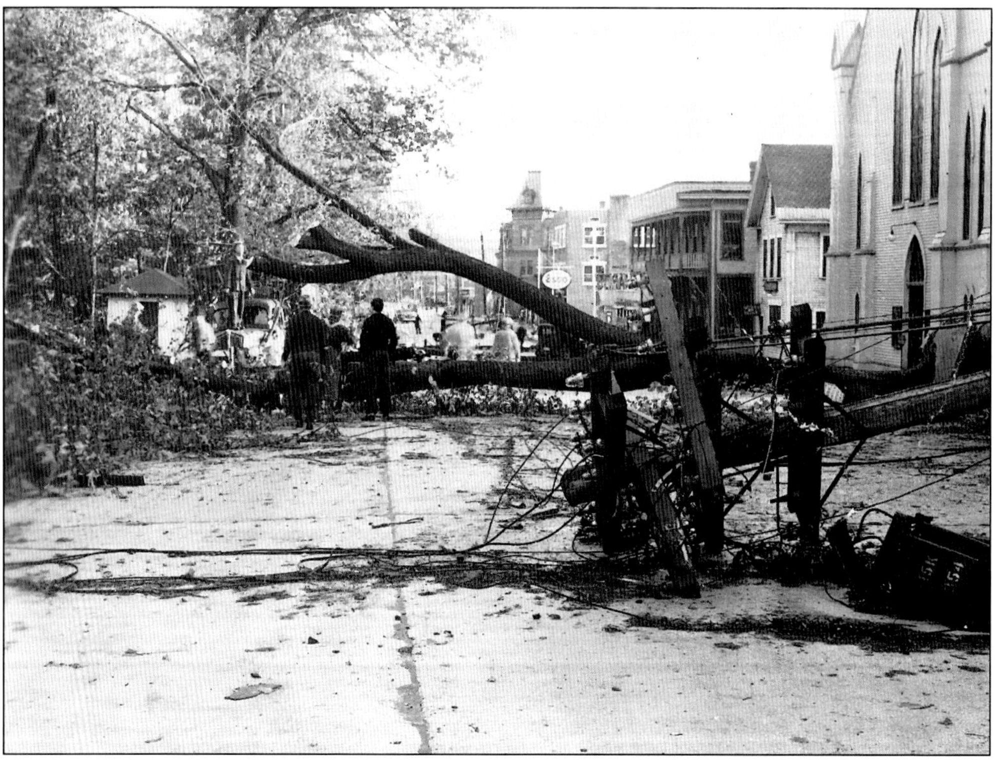

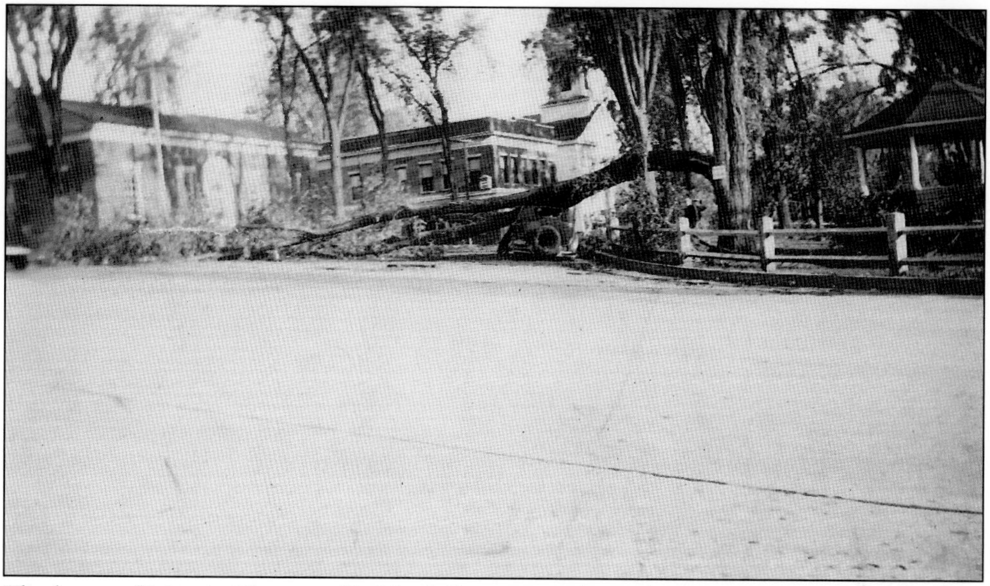

The home of Minnie Chase on Highland Street, just above the Common, was the scene of a near fatality because of one of the huge elm trees that fell. A man sitting in the car under the elm that toppled escaped with minor scratches.

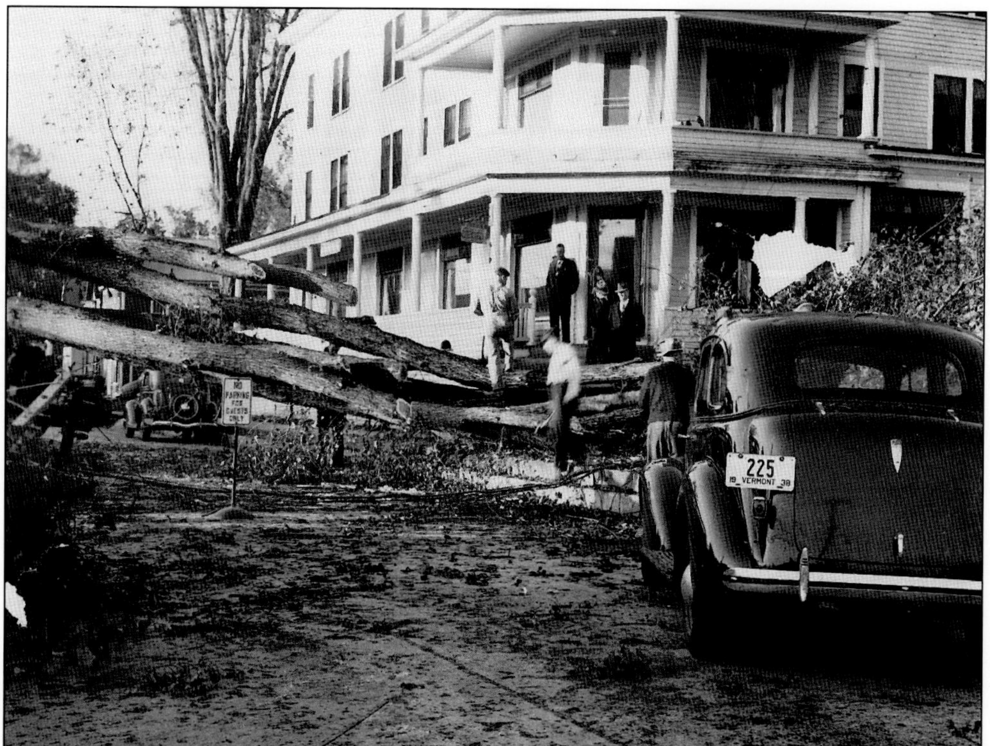

As in many parts of town, trees which fell to the winds, like these near the Plymouth Inn on South Main Street, blocked the roads for many hours until crews could clear them.

ACKNOWLEDGMENTS

The Plymouth Historical Society wishes to acknowledge the time and effort of the committee that selected and arranged the photographs from the Society's collection for this publication: William and Elizabeth Batchelder, Eleanor Fuller, Robert Olmstead, Jenny Smialek, and Elsa Turmelle. Special thanks to Mary Crowley for her time, advice, and encouragement, to Katherine Hillier for her technical expertise, and to Tom and Dorothy Anderson, Ross Deachman, Fletcher Adams of the Pemigewasset National Bank, and Speare Memorial Hospital for photographs, which they kindly made available to us for inclusion in this book.